IMAGES
of America

NEEDHAM

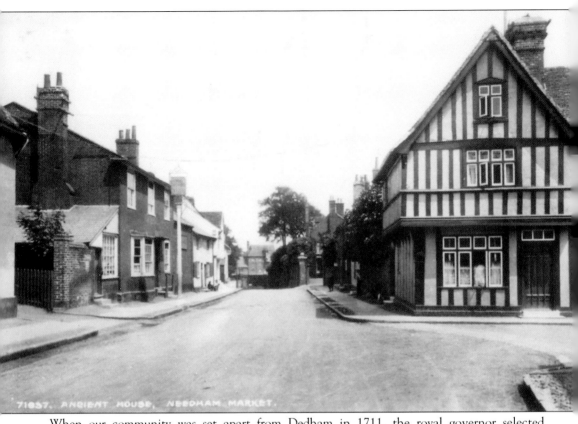

When our community was set apart from Dedham in 1711, the royal governor selected Needham as the name for the new town because near Dedham in England was the ancient town of Needham Market. That English town has many medieval and Tudor buildings of historic interest and is still a thriving East Anglian community. It is very hospitable to our citizens when they visit.

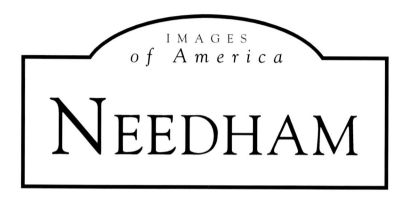
IMAGES of America
NEEDHAM

The Needham Historical Society, Inc.

ARCADIA
PUBLISHING

Copyright © 1997 by The Needham Historical Society, Inc.
ISBN 978-0-7385-6546-0

Published by Arcadia Publishing
Charleston, South Carolina

Printed in the United States of America

Library of Congress Catalog Card Number: 2008942219

For all general information contact Arcadia Publishing at:
Telephone 843-853-2070
Fax 843-853-0044
E-mail sales@arcadiapublishing.com
For customer service and orders:
Toll-Free 1-888-313-2665

Visit us on the Internet at www.arcadiapublishing.com

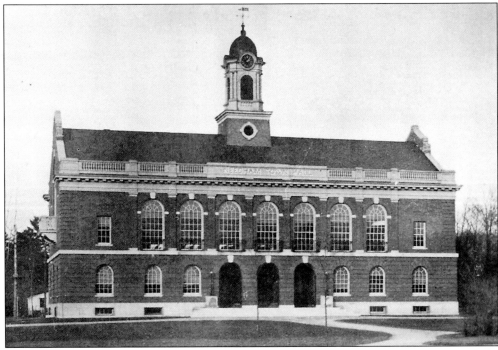

Needham Town Hall, dedicated September 2, 1902, stands as the dominant feature of the Needham Town Common Historic District, which was placed on the National Register of Historic Places through the actions of the Needham Historical Commission. This imposing Georgian Colonial Revival-style building once housed the town's auditorium on the second floor, the site of town meetings for fifty years. The building is now completely devoted to town administrative office use.

Contents

Acknowledgments		6
Introduction		7
1.	Our Farming Past	9
2.	Notable Needhamites	19
3.	Needham at Work	33
4.	Events That Shaped Our Town	49
5.	Our Architectural History	73
6.	Around Our Town	97

Acknowledgments

Editorial Committee:
Carol Johnson Boulris, Author and Editor
Henry F. Hicks Jr., Historian and Curator, Needham Historical Society
Pauline Merrill Attridge, Archivist, Needham Historical Society
Elizabeth Lewis Rich, Member, Needham Historical Commission

Special Appreciation to:
Ann MacFate, Director, Needham Free Public Library; Arian Schuster, Archivist, Needham Free Public Library; Leslie G. Crumbaker, Needham History Expert; Naomi Anderson, MotoPhoto; Marvin Rosenkrantz, Needham Camera Shop; Joanne Attridge, Computer Consultant; and those individuals who have contributed to Needham's history.

Photographic Sources:
Archives of the Needham Historical Society; Archives of the Needham Free Public Library; Collection of the late Laurence Welsh (Lorraine Welsh); Collection of the late Ruth Latham (Mr. and Mrs. George Krech); James Hugh Powers; Collection of Robert Chalue, Photographer; Marion Lebourveau and Needham Girl Scouts; Elvira Castano Palmerio; Roche Bros. Supermarkets; Needham Fire Department and Donald Ingram; Needham Police Department; the Wyeth Family; Clifford Kinne; *The Needham Tab* newspaper; *The Needham Times* newspaper; William L. Sweet; Amy Hicks; and The Dawson Collection (James Turbayne).

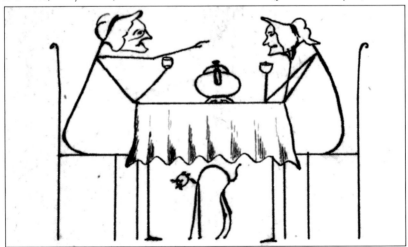

This book is dedicated to Needham residents who, over decades, have served the town as volunteers and to the organizations that have made this "Our Town." Volunteers have given time and energies to governmental boards, social agencies, the library, the hospital, the historical society, and churches. This logo of the Tea and Toast Club, a literary society that existed from 1886 to the 1940s, is a reminder of the variety of clubs, associations, and societies that have attracted Needhamites. Their names and interests have changed throughout the years but their importance to the quality of life here continues.

Introduction

The development of the town of Needham began in the 1640s when the area was first explored by colonists. Settlers brought cattle here to graze in the 1670s. In 1681 the lands of present-day Needham and Wellesley were purchased from Massachusetts Indian tribal leader William Nehoiden for £10, 40 shillings worth of corn, and 50 acres of land in Newton at Hemlock Gorge for hunting and fishing. The transaction later provided the theme for the Needham Town Seal. A large portion of this area was called the Great Plain or the Charles River Valley. The Indians called the river "Quinobequin," "river that turns upon itself," because the Charles makes many turns as it encompasses Needham in a moat-like configuration.

Our Colonial history is that of a poor farming community located off the main roads, distrustful of both the morals and government of Boston and afraid of the French and Indian raiders.

By 1711 there were more than fifty families here. They found it difficult and too time-consuming to travel to the town center in Dedham for trading, church, and town meetings, so they petitioned for separation. On November 5 of that year, the town of Needham was incorporated and was then composed of two villages: West Needham (centered near the current Wellesley Square) and East Needham (at the junction of Central Avenue and Nehoiden Street). A meetinghouse, which was also the place of worship, was built at East Needham Centre; and the town of Needham began. By 1718, the town voted to keep three "moving schooles," which could be pulled to various locations by oxen. These were succeeded by schools in homes and in rented buildings before real schools were constructed. Progress was being made in the development of the town.

The American Revolution came to Needham dramatically, as 185 men from our three militia companies responded to the Lexington battle of April 19, 1775. Few, if any, able-bodied men remained in town. Subsequently, many other Needhamites served in the War for Independence under General George Washington, including the distinguished officer, political leader, and town father, Colonel William McIntosh.

Until the arrival of the railroads in 1853, the center of town was along Central Avenue at Nehoiden Street. From then on, the gradual move of the town's center to the Great Plain Village was necessitated by the fact that the Charles River Railroad did not come to the old village. In the 1870s, when the First Parish Church was hauled to its current location in Needham Center, only the Old Burying Ground and the 1720 parsonage were left as reminders of the original settlement.

The people of the town made a modest living as farmers, although horticulture and dairying eventually became prominent. Highlandville (now Needham Heights) took on a completely different character with the 1850s immigration of English knitters such as William Carter and Mark Lee. What started as cottage industries developed into large knitting factories that produced world-famous knit goods.

Within ten days of the attack on Fort Sumter in 1861, posters appeared all over town summoning citizens to enlist with the cry, "NEEDHAM TO THE RESCUE!" During the War of the Rebellion, more than four hundred area men were credited with service. Our citizens responded to the wars of the twentieth century as well: World War I involved four hundred men; World War II, seventeen hundred men and women; the Korean War, six hundred men and women; the Vietnam War, over three hundred men and women; and Desert Storm, thirty-six men and women.

Almost from the beginning, the western part of the town was dissatisfied with the location of town government. This culminated in the separation of Wellesley from Needham in 1881, which divided Needham approximately in half. The town poor farm was included in the division, the site later becoming the Wellesley Country Club. It was not until the turn of the century, after a new high school and a new town hall had been built and several trolley lines were in operation, that Needham began to gain the momentum that made it a successful suburban community.

Gradually both dairy farming and the knitting industry declined. In 1955 the well-known Walker-Gordon Dairy Farm closed and in 1988 even the world-famous Carter Company relocated. The creation, however, of one of New England's first industrial parks in 1950, the later development of high-technology firms along Route 128 (the nation's first circumferential highway around a major city—Boston), the improvement of railroad passenger service to Boston, and the excellent reputation of Needham schools have contributed to the town's emergence as one of the most desirable suburbs of Boston. Retention of the representative town meeting form of government, tree-lined streets with attractive residential neighborhoods, the small-town ambiance in our organizations and shopping areas, and many fine places of worship all help to evoke the feeling of a typical New England town.

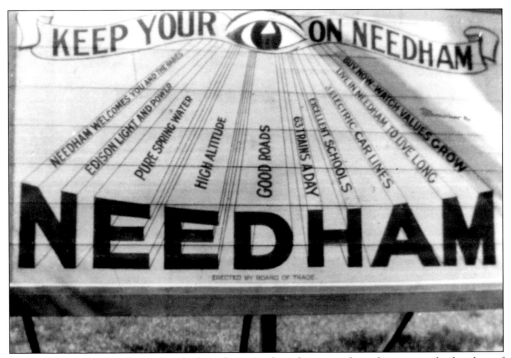

In the 1920s, the Needham Board of Trade erected road signs such as this one at the borders of the town, hoping to attract new residents and businesses.

One
Our Farming Past

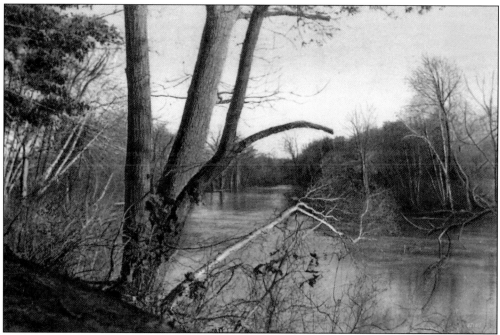

Needham's first industry was the making of brush brooms and fagots. Called "Needham currency," in Colonial times the fagots were transported by ox team to Boston and exchanged for household supplies or sold to the bakeries and coastal shipping enterprises of the area for fuel. The fagots were bundles of a plant that grew along the marshy edges of the Charles River. They generated great heat and were nearly ashless when burned.

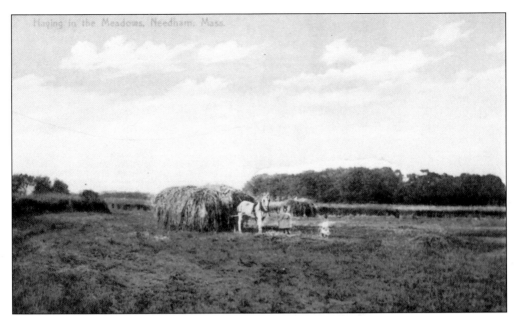

From the earliest days of the town, Needham farmers found it necessary to specialize their efforts, due to the poor glacial soil of the area. Because cattle raising was the main Colonial undertaking of rural Boston, our farmers grew hay for the food and bedding required by the animals.

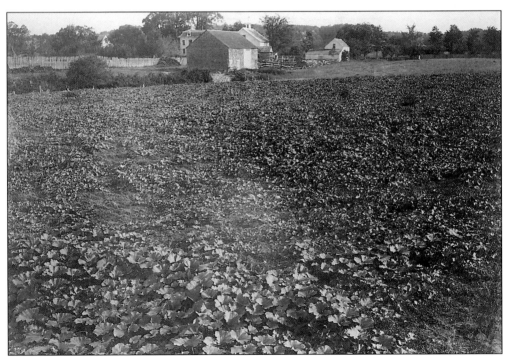

As better transportation to Boston developed by the late nineteenth century, some successful, large market gardens were able to serve a larger area. On Great Plain Avenue near today's Babson College, the James Mackintosh farm grew beets, pumpkins, beans, corn, celery, onions, carrots, tomatoes, melons, parsnips, squash, potatoes, and cucumbers.

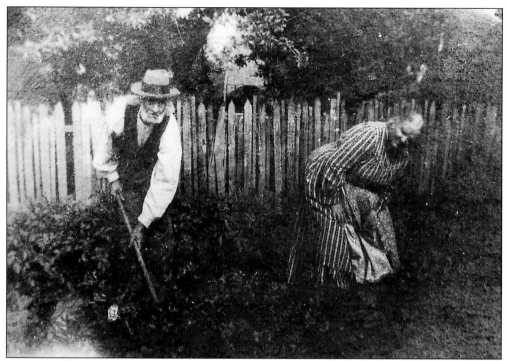

Most Needhamites were non-affluent, self-sufficient farmers who kept well-tended home gardens into the late nineteenth century. Produce from a garden such as this was used in a partial barter economy. Here Harriet and Deacon Cyrus Upham were busy at work at the turn of the century.

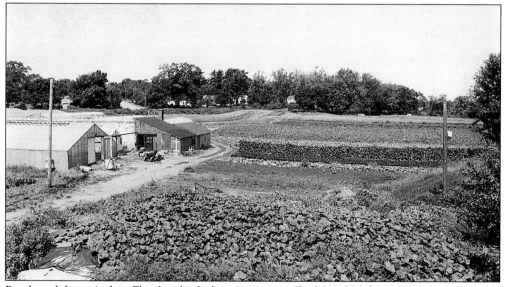

Purchased from Arthur Fletcher by Italian immigrant Ferdinand Volante, Volante's Farm on Central Avenue is the last remaining working farm in Needham. It is situated on land that has been tilled since the early 1700s when it belonged to Robert Fuller, who was among the first settlers. Volante's Farm remains a major provider of fresh produce, vegetable seedlings, and flowering plants for our residents today.

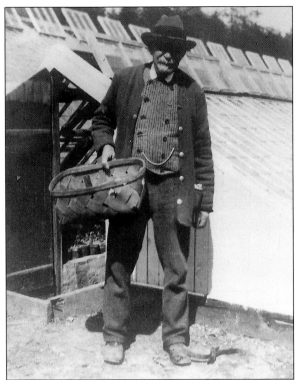

Swiss-born naturalist Denys Zirngiebel retired from the Arnold Arboretum of Harvard University in the 1860s and purchased 35 acres of land along the Charles River on South Street. Introducing horticulture to Needham, he developed a major business and shipped flowers weekly to the White House and U.S. State Department. He was the first to cultivate the giant Swiss pansy in America. The farm was all sold off by the 1920s.

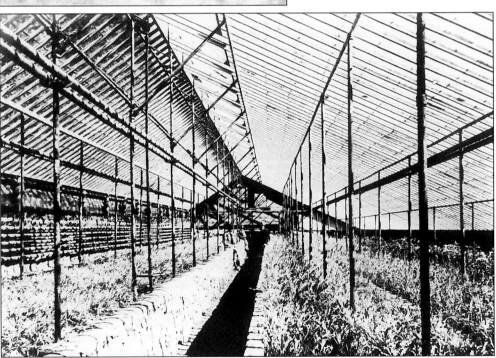

Denys Zirngiebel held the patents for a number of innovative and successful greenhouse heating systems. He won prizes for his methods, as well as recognition for the quality of his plants. Zirngiebel's daughter Henrietta was the mother of artist N.C. Wyeth.

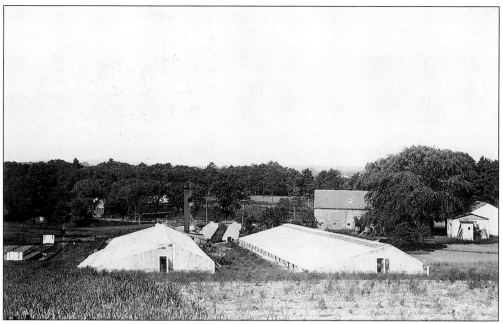

By the early 1900s, this hill, which is now the site of Needham High School, was occupied by extensive greenhouses owned by the Richwagen family. The base of the hill was cut away to form Memorial Park in 1921.

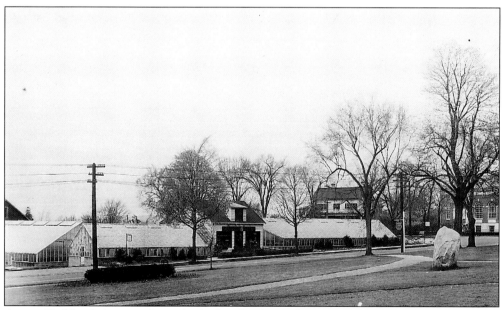

Across Highland Avenue from the high school, on the site of the current Sudbury Farms Market, the Richwagens later operated a retail florist shop and additional greenhouses. It was one of many local florists (located also on Bird's Hill, Maple Street, and Great Plain Avenue) that supplied Boston institutions and flower markets.

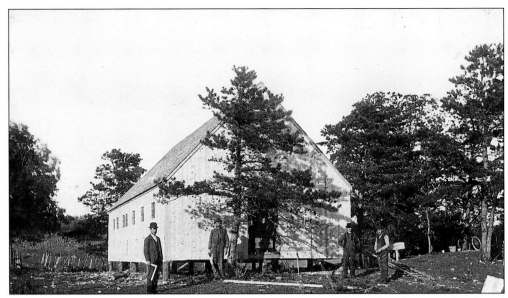

The subject of how to control the large swine population of Needham often dominated Colonial and nineteenth-century town meetings. Members at one session voted to impound the swine and at a subsequent session to allow them to run free. Here, in 1893, a piggery was built for Henry Blackman on Greendale Avenue.

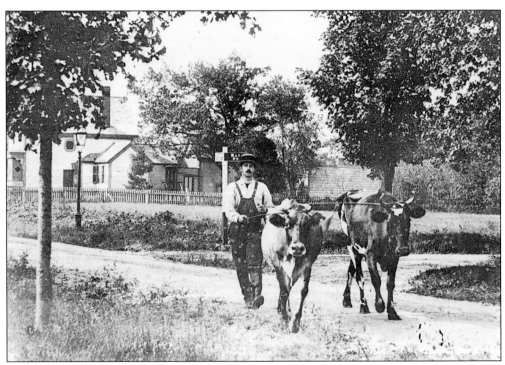

From the earliest times, local farmers kept cattle to meet family needs. Howard Tisdale, c. 1890, continued that tradition and walked his cows at the corner of Webster and May Streets. Note the kerosene street lamp, one of many placed in the town in 1883. These were replaced about ten years later by electric lights.

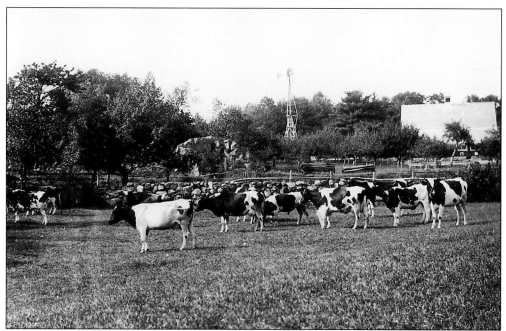

By the 1900s, Needham had more than eight dairies supplying milk to the area. This herd, pastured in a field on a local farm near South Street and Dedham Avenue, illustrated the pastoral and rustic character of the town.

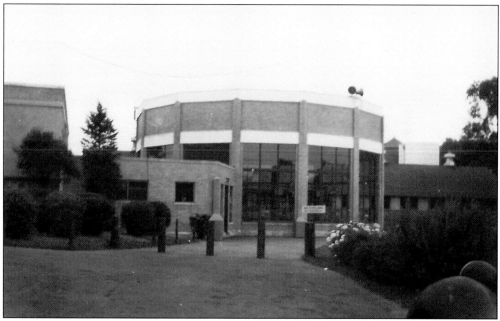

In 1891, George Walker, Boston owner of a lithograph company, and Gustavus Gordon, scientist, formed Walker-Gordon Laboratories to develop processes for the prevention of contamination of milk and to answer the call by enlightened physicians for better babies' milk formulas. This plant was located in the Charles River Village section of Needham, with another large facility in New Jersey.

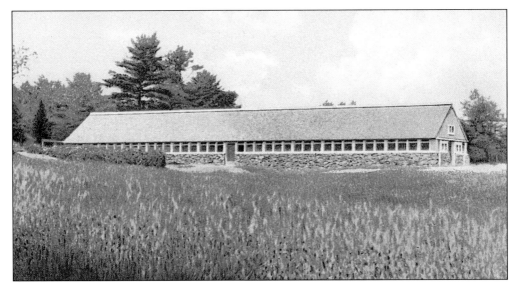

The Walker-Gordon barn housed more than four hundred milk cows of the highest quality. Hundreds of acres of land were devoted to their care. Walker-Gordon also operated a popular ice cream parlor. The nearby Walker Lane, Walker Pond, and Walker-Gordon playing fields of today memorialize this enterprise. One barn of the large complex remains on Fisher Street and is used by the local animal control officer.

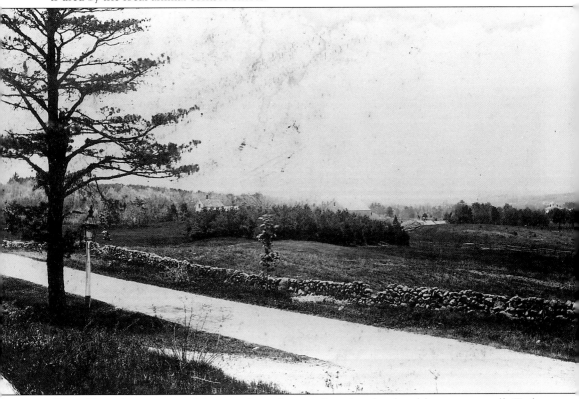

Great Plain Avenue wound its way through a rural setting, bordered by a stone wall. Today the area is occupied by the Needham Golf Club course, developed in the 1920s, and by private

The scientific dairy production facilities of the Walker-Gordon Dairy Farm were widely advertised and utilized modern advancements in the handling of milk products.

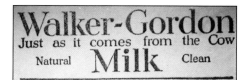

What Walker-Gordon service means

By controlling both production and distribution, Walker-Gordon Co. are enabled to give customers an unusual protection. We raise many of our own cows and keep them under constant supervision. Milking is done under the most sanitary conditions, — followed by quick cooling, bottling, double-capping and packing in ice for delivery.

Then this milk — perfectly produced — is distributed by our own wagons and trucks. At every step in production and distribution Walker-Gordon Milk is under personal control. We deliver our customers regularly. Let us put you on our list for Milk, Cream or Buttermilk. Telephone your order today.

Also Cream, Buttermilk and Modified Milk

Walker-Gordon Farms
CHARLES RIVER

Orders may be given by phone (Farms) Needham 0330 R; Needham 0112 M; (Boston office) Kenmore 3670. Also to

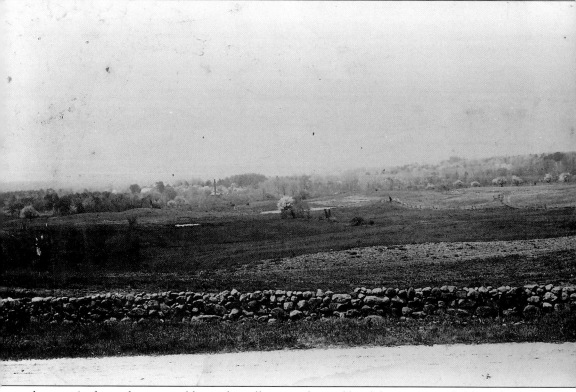

homes. As far as the eye could see, the rolling meadows of local farms surrounded large barns and farmhouses. Such was the scene in pre-1890 Needham.

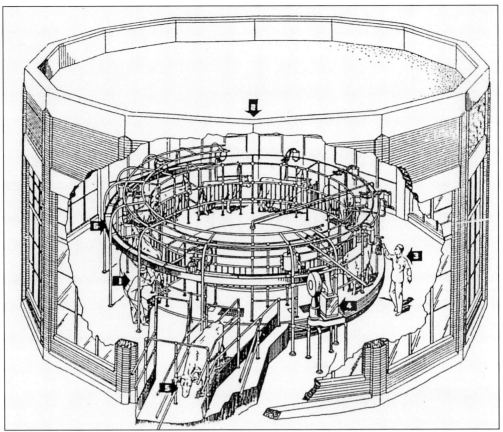

This rotolactor was the crown jewel of the world-famous Walker-Gordon Dairy. Moving 10 feet per minute and making a revolution every 10 minutes, the machine washed, dried, and milked ten cows at a time. No hands touched the milk and everything that did touch it was washed and sterilized between milkings. Milk went from cow to bottle with limited exposure to air. This rotolactor, displayed at the 1939 New York World's Fair, was subsequently used by the Borden Company.

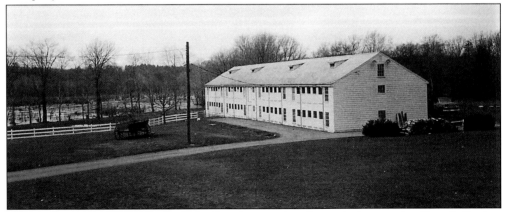

Among the remaining vestiges of Needham's agricultural past is the popular Owen's Poultry Farm, pictured here in 1979. Started in 1935 by Walter and Elizabeth Owen, it is operated today by the third generation of the family.

Two
Notable Needhamites

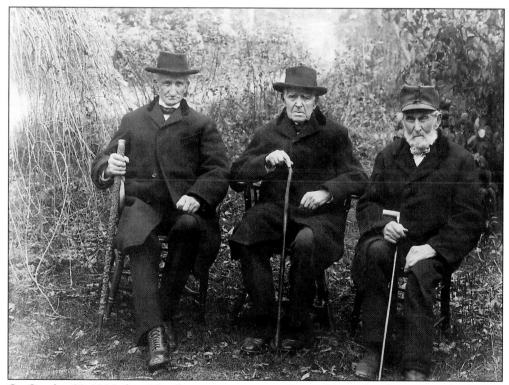

On October 30, 1906, three Needham nonagenarians, George Hiram Gay (age ninety-four), Enos Tucker (age ninety-nine), and Ezra Fuller (age ninety-one), posed while reminiscing at Fuller's home. All were born and spent their entire lives in Needham, where they were farmers.

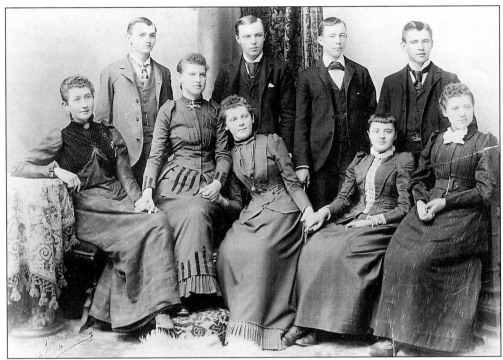

Nine young people comprised the Needham High School graduating class of 1881, in great contrast to our recent classes of two hundred to over six hundred during the peak years of the school. This 1881 class was large for the early days and is noteworthy for the large number of males included. Their future occupations included physician, teacher, bookkeeper, mail clerk, and household worker.

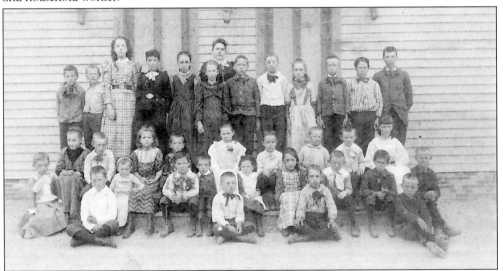

Daughter of a local farmer, Miss Mary Glancy taught many generations of Needham children. She stood in June 1893 behind the back row, with future artist N.C. Wyeth in front of her left arm. First teaching at the old Harris School, she was later its principal. Wyeth presented one of his paintings in her honor to the new Harris School. Now at the local library, this painting, *A Fine Boy and His Mother*, is signed "NCW to Mary Glancy."

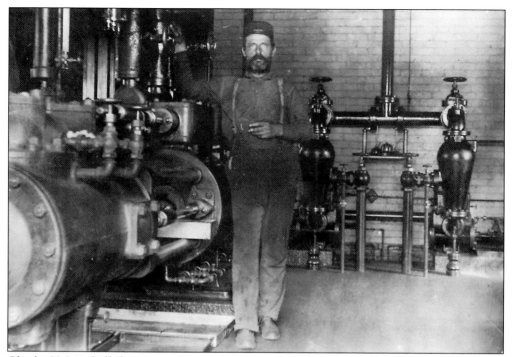

Charles H. Mitchell, former cavalryman, Westerner, and the town's water department engineer, was pictured at the pumping station on Dedham Avenue near South Street and the reservoir. During construction of the town's water pipe system, Mitchell uncovered many American Indian artifacts such as arrow points and implements, which he donated to form the nucleus of the Eastern Woodland Indian collection now on display at the Needham Historical Society.

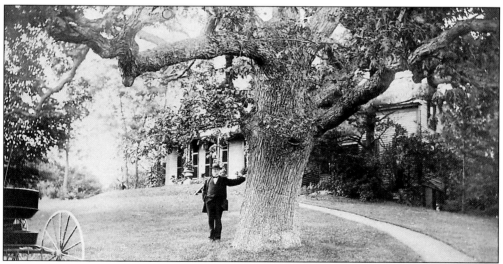

On Nehoiden Street were the house and oak tree of C.C. Greenwood, town clerk, who died in 1897. He was also selectman, assessor, and representative to the General Court. An antiquarian, he collected nineteenth-century political and town notices now at the Needham Historical Society and transcribed a book of epitaphs from the Old Burying Ground. This tree was vigorous until 1908 when it succumbed to rot. The society has a gavel made from its wood.

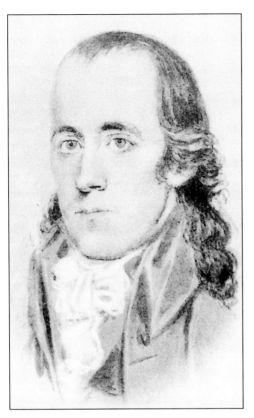

Third minister of the First Parish Church, the Reverend Stephen Palmer was the town's first historian and a member of the Massachusetts Historical Society. A Harvard graduate, he entered the ministry in 1792 and served until his death in 1821 at age fifty-five. His sermon delivered on the occasion of the Needham Centennial is considered the town's first history. An elementary school was named for him in 1914.

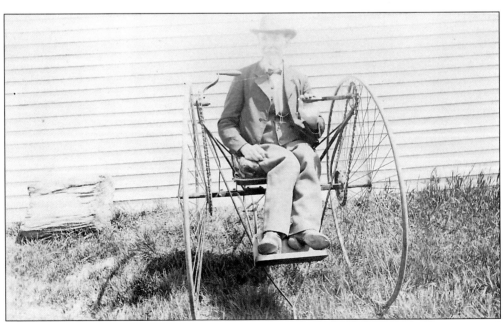

This gentleman, a Needham cobbler, was crippled in one leg. He used this contraption to travel from his home to his place of business. The picture was taken by Emery Coulter, who owned the mobile photographic studio pictured on p. 43.

Dr. Josiah Noyes was the first graduate of a medical school (Dartmouth, 1825) to practice in Needham. He had wide knowledge of herbs, assisted in a town map survey by measuring the roads with a device on the wheel of his chaise, and was a member of the school committee. Noyes Park, near his home and in the McIntosh Historic District, was named for him. His desk, papers, and instruments are at the historical society.

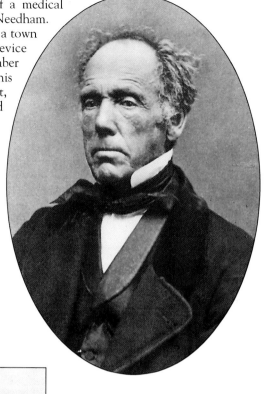

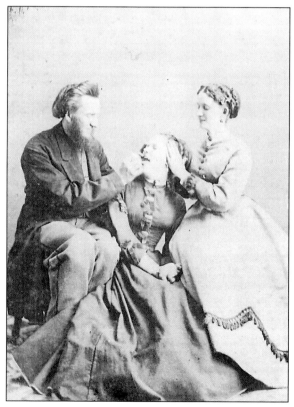

Drs. Vesta and Albert Miller practiced here. Albert, a graduate of the University of Pennsylvania, came to Needham in 1876. He was also involved in real estate, developing the Oakland Avenue area. Vesta, beloved as a physician, was called "skillful, faithful, and self-sacrificing." She was a temperance leader who held W.C.T.U. meetings at her home. A graduate of the College of Physicians and Surgeons in Boston, she practiced for more than thirty years.

In 1899, Miss Elizabeth Willgoose announced that she was ready to undertake the care of patients in her home, The Verandahs. She graduated from Boston City Hospital Training School for Nurses and stated she was "prepared to give the most careful attention to her work, carrying out directions as minutely and conscientiously as could be done in a hospital, while still keeping the daintiness and cheerfulness of a home."

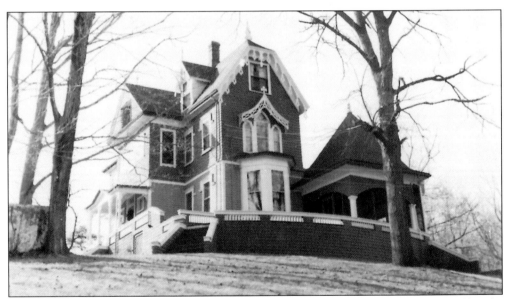

Miss Willgoose's home sanitarium, The Verandahs, was located on a Central Avenue hill at the rear of the old McIntosh Tavern site, now Nehoiden Glen Condominiums. Her advertisement stated: "It is perfect in its sanitary arrangements, is surrounded by wide verandahs on three of its sides, its lawns are large and well kept, the rooms are sunny and airy, and altogether her house is well planned to give comfort and restfulness to an invalid."

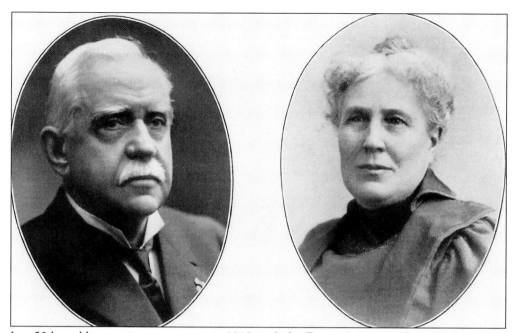

In a 50th wedding anniversary picture in 1918 are Judge Emery Grover and his wife, the former Lydia Orr, daughter of Needham manufacturer Galen Orr. The present Needham Public Schools administration building, which was the former high school (1898), now bears Emery Grover's name, honoring this prominent judge and local official who also served as selectman and school committee member.

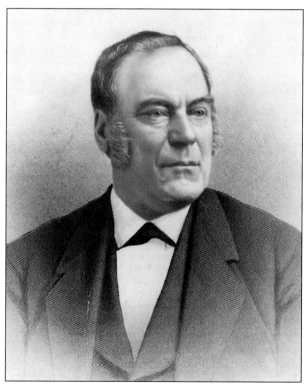

One important nineteenth-century Needham resident was Galen Orr, owner of a large blind hinge and fastenings factory, established in 1839 on Rosemary Creek. His factory supplied much of the hardware for the new construction in Boston's Back Bay. The only Grand Army of the Republic (GAR) post in the country to honor a civilian was named for Mr. Orr, due to his care and concern as a selectman for Civil War soldiers and their families.

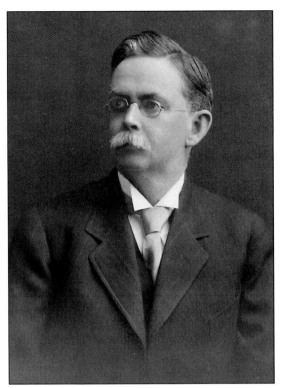

The second significant historian of the town was George Kuhn Clarke, who wrote and published the 1911 *History of Needham* for the town's bicentennial. This 746-page tome was a masterpiece of historical detail. A distinguished Boston attorney-at-law, Clarke owned the 1720 Townsend House on Central Avenue and served on numerous town committees, including the library board of trustees.

An important manufacturer of silk and elastic stockings, knit surgical bandages, and underwear was William G. Moseley, who also served as town moderator for twenty-eight town meetings from 1899 to 1911. An incorporator of the Needham Cooperative Bank in 1902, Moseley was admitted to the Massachusetts Bar in 1907 and served as town auditor, selectman, and school committee member.

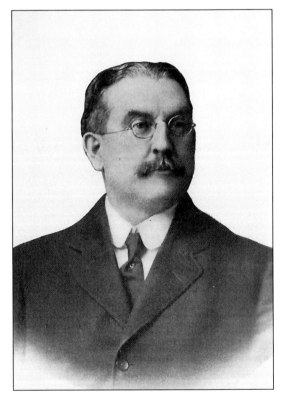

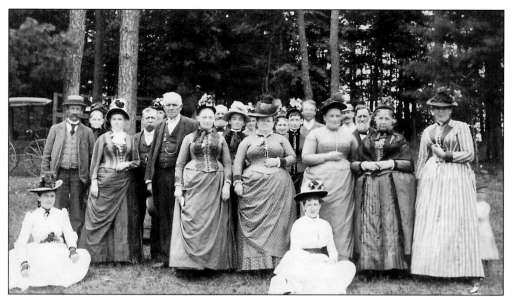

The Needhamites on a picnic in 1889 in their best picnic attire included Mrs. Andrew Newell Wyeth standing on the far right of the front row. Peeking from behind her skirts is her son, who later attained fame as artist N.C. Wyeth.

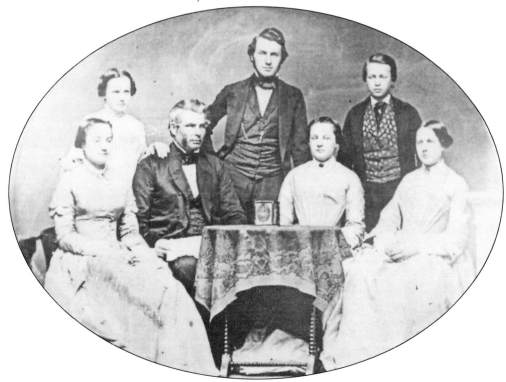

Lemuel Lyon and family gathered for this picture c. 1850. Lyon owned the Needham Hat Manufacturing Company. In 1834 he built the dam that formed Rosemary Lake in the area formerly known as Rosemary Meadow. One of Lyon's sons died in Japan, where he was serving as U.S. Consul. Another family member, a dentist, developed Lyon's Tooth Powder.

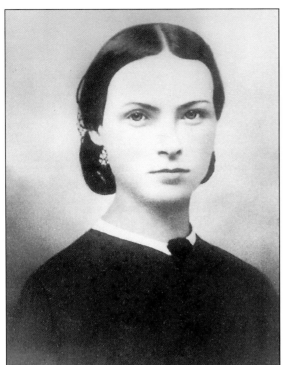

Martha Lee Carter was the second wife of William Carter. They had four children—William H., Mary Elizabeth, John James, and Horace Albert. Martha Carter was the sister of John and Mark Lee, with whom Carter later went into business partnership.

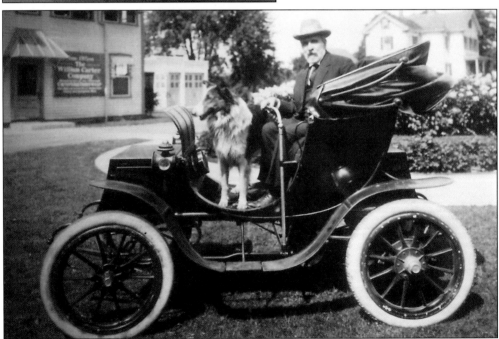

William Carter came to the United States from England in 1857 and built a large knitwear manufacturing company of international repute. He gave generously to the town, donating land for two libraries, two churches, and a cricket field, and was one of the first manufacturers to adopt the Saturday half-holiday. During World War II, in 1942, his sons donated his 1910 horseless carriage to the local salvage committee in support of the war effort.

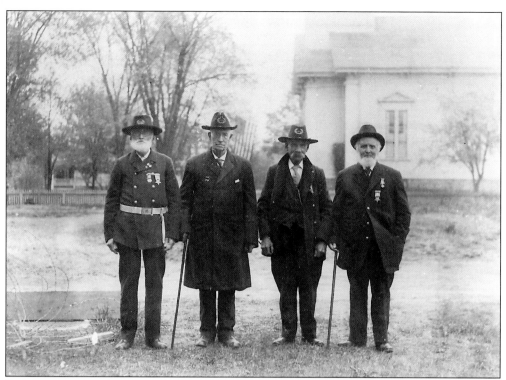

Just prior to 1917 when one of these proud gentlemen died, Needham's last few remaining Civil War veterans stood with the First Parish Church in the background. More than four hundred Needham residents served in the Union Army, including Lyman Wilcox, Paul Hutchinson, William Bell, and William Horrocks, whose medals and uniforms were worn with pride.

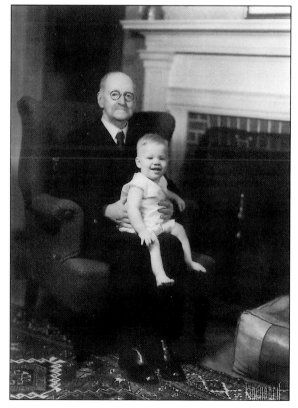

Moving here from Stoughton, George W. Southworth started the first permanent local newspaper, *The Needham Chronicle*, in 1874. Shown here with a great-grandson, Southworth remained editor and publisher into the 1930s, did most of the town's printing, and served as librarian and library treasurer. He was known "to use good type and a higher grade of paper than usual." The newspaper retained the *Chronicle* name until 1997.

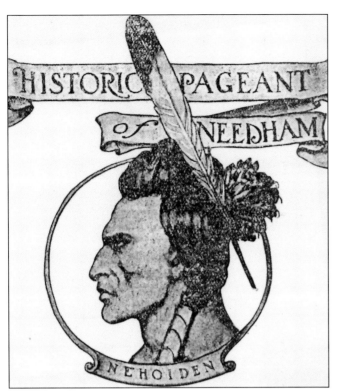

Recognized leader of the local Massachusetts Indians, and most mentioned Indian in Massachusetts Bay Colony records, William Nehoiden negotiated the treaty with Dedham planters for the purchase of the land of present-day Needham and Wellesley. Nehoiden became a Christian and worked with the Reverend Mr. John Eliot on the translation of the Holy Bible into the Indian tongue. This illustration by N.C. Wyeth was drawn for the New Century Club.

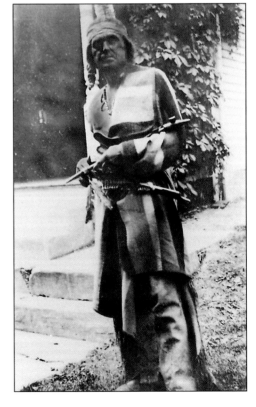

Stimson Wyeth, brother of N.C. Wyeth, portrayed Nehoiden for an enactment of the Needham Town Seal in the 1920s. Often a model for his brother's works, Stimson was a distinguished educator in Boston high schools as a teacher of English and was active in Needham cultural and civic affairs.

Starting her political career in 1924 as a member of the board of health and later an elected selectman, Leslie B. Cutler was a representative to the Massachusetts General Court (1936–1948) and state senator (1949–1968). A distinguished twentieth-century citizen of Needham, her interests in aviation, mental health, correction system reform, and conservation made her a "woman ahead of her time." Mother of five, she lived from 1890 to 1971.

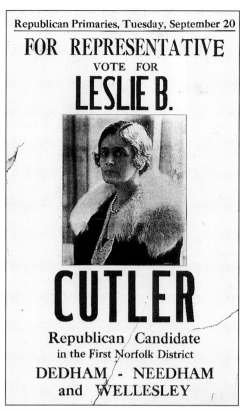

Active in the Red Cross and the Needham Historical Society, Mrs. Cutler was director and thirty-year president of the Needham Community Council. It was said that "no worthwhile project was ever turned down by Mrs. Cutler. She has done so many things for so many people." Stephanie Kalin, shown here with Mrs. Cutler (turning in a volunteer's report form), later served as director of the community council.

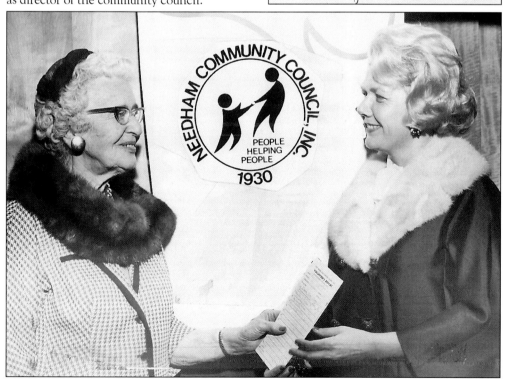

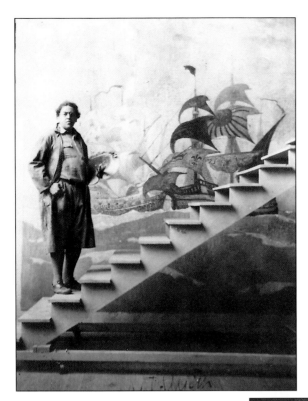

Newell Convers Wyeth was born in Needham in 1882 and attended Needham public schools. His earliest work was magazine illustration, from which he moved into book illustration. Through his pictures, particularly those in children's classics, he reached a greater audience than perhaps any other illustrator. He was also a distinguished muralist and landscape artist. Wyeth died near his home in Chadds Ford, Pennsylvania, in 1945 due to a train accident at the peak of his career.

In 1971, at age seventy-four, Giovanni Castano, renowned muralist and art restorer, repaired the water-damaged murals in the Massachusetts State House. For this work he received a governor's citation. Born in Gasperina, Italy, and a Needham resident from the early 1930s until his death in 1978, Castano also maintained a studio and gallery on Newbury Street in Boston. A prominent appraiser and dealer in fine arts, he was known as a painter of landscapes.

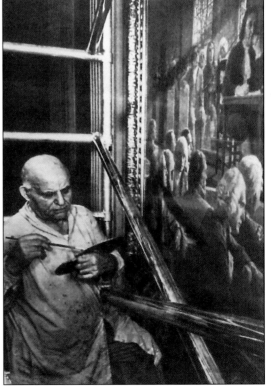

Three
Needham at Work

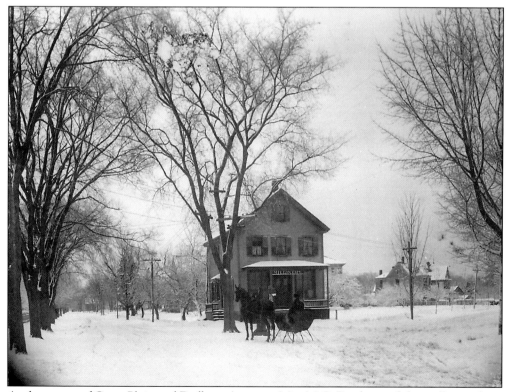

At the corner of Great Plain and Dedham Avenues, Miss M.C. Boyd owned this millinery shop. Her business was one of three hat shops for women in that era (post-1885 but pre-1898 when the trolley tracks were laid).

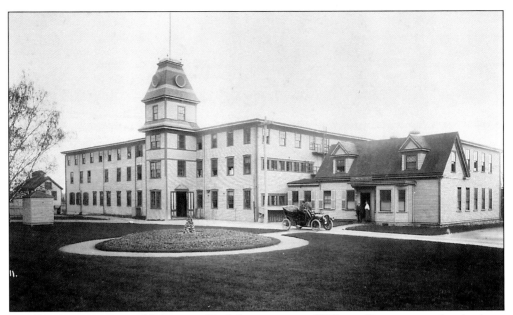

Needham's most successful knitter, English immigrant William Carter, started a business in his home in 1865. By 1870 he owned a small factory and c. 1875 bought the rectangular Lee Company building, the nucleus of Carter Mill #1, shown here. The Carter Company prospered with seven plants, eventually producing 40 million garments yearly. In the early 1950s, the manufacturing department moved to the South. This building became the corporate headquarters until the company was sold in 1988.

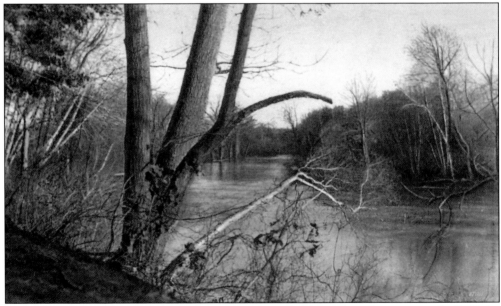

William Carter had leased this building on Rosemary Lake to a bicycle company. In 1902 the several hundred knitting machines of Carter's were moved to this factory, Carter Mill #2 or Lower Mill. Three knitting companies had previously used the facility, built in 1866 on the site of Galen Orr's batting mill. The property later housed the Tillotson Rubber Company and then became the site of a large apartment complex.

Pictured here are two foot-worked Lee knitting frames, dating back at least to the early 1800s, which were brought to Needham from England by Midland knitters who settled here. The frames were later used to make surgical stockings. The metal needles indicate the elastic-thread process invented by a Needham man, George Freeman. Both pieces of equipment are displayed at the Needham Historical Society.

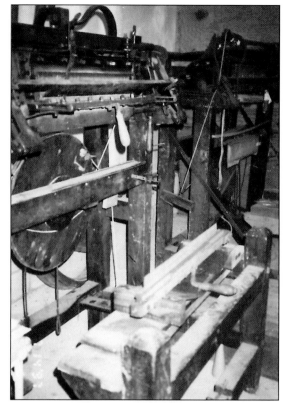

In 1906, women were at work in the sewing room of the Saxony Knitting Mills in Needham Heights. This was a typical scene in the large mills, of which there were several in town in the latter half of the nineteenth century.

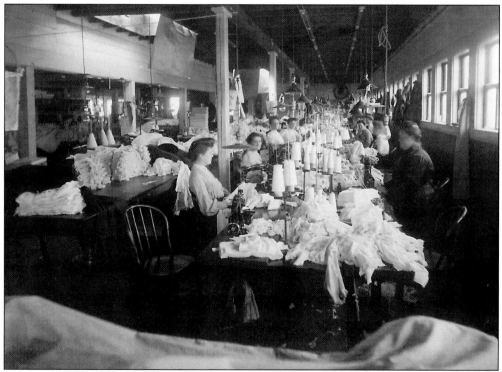

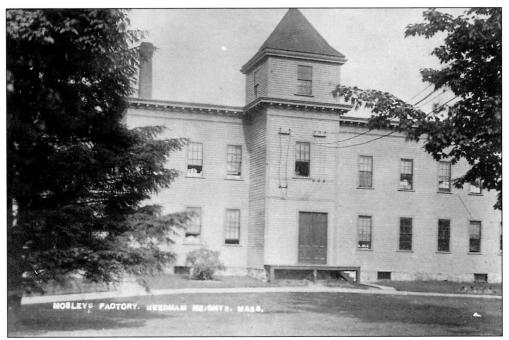

Moseley and Company, manufacturers of knitwear including children's Tiny-Wear items, was established in 1883. This company, Highland Mills, a major competitor of the Carter Company, was located on Highland Avenue in Needham Heights (Highlandville) opposite Carter's building.

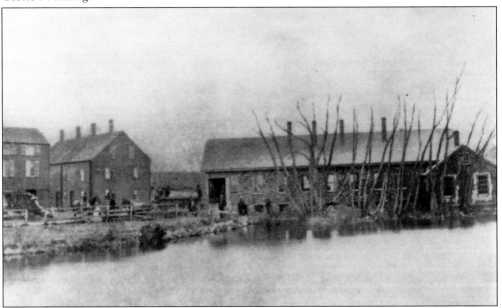

Galen Orr's Blind Hinge Factory was located on Rosemary Creek. In 1839, with a forge at his Central Avenue house, Orr began the manufacture of blind hinges and fastenings. In 1844 he opened his factory, a major supplier of hardware used in the new Back Bay area of Boston. Orr also ran a gristmill and a mill for cotton batting and was a selectman and member of the state legislature.

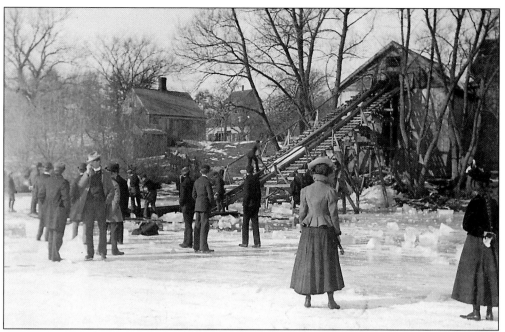

Before the invention of artificial refrigeration, several private ice companies made use of Blacksmith and Rosemary Ponds. Blacksmith Pond was a large, shallow body of water extending between Great Plain Avenue and Nehoiden Street. In the 1930s the pond was drained by directing Rosemary Brook into a culvert. Current streets in the Blacksmith Drive and Meadowbrook Drive areas were built on the drained acreage.

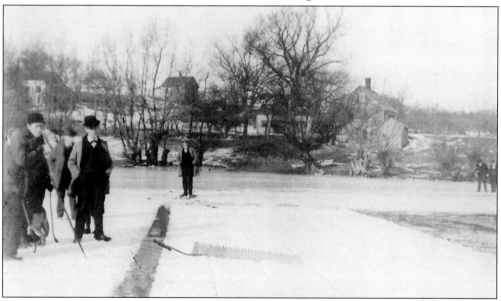

Rosemary Lake was formed by water from Rosemary Brook, which ran from the area behind the current Roche Bros. Market to Oak Street, Perry Drive, and Gay Street, and off the hill at Trout Pond. An 1888 advertisement stated that "no impure water runs into the pond." By February, when the ice had thickened to a foot or more, ice merchants were ready for the annual harvest. The ice was cut into slabs, then cubes, and stored in straw.

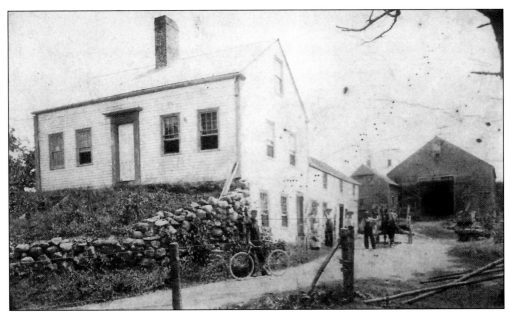

The old McIntosh house at 1386 Great Plain Avenue was the site of several businesses. In the rear ell was a glue factory and later a shoe shop. Between the ell and the barn was the original meat market. Later an ice business was run from this property, using ice from McIntosh Pond, later called Trout Pond. This pond was man-made by McIntosh, who dammed a brook running through his land.

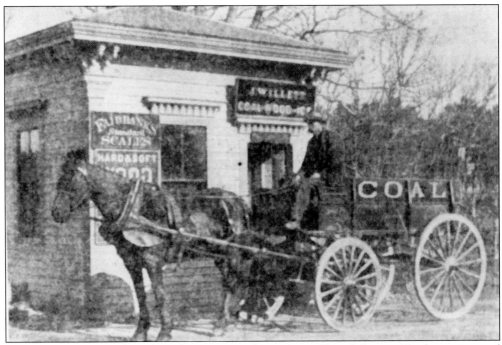

J. Willett's coal, wood, and ice business was located on Chapel Street. His large sign and advertisement, painted on the side of a brick building, can still be seen in a small alley leading off Great Plain Avenue.

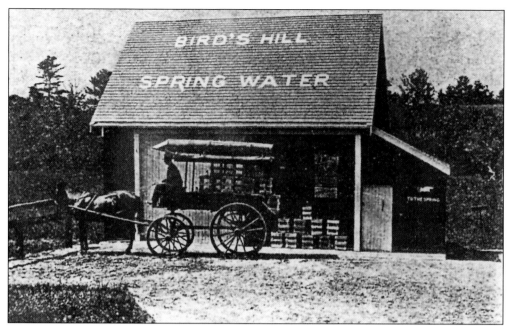

In 1789, President George Washington passed through Needham. Met at the town line by Colonel William McIntosh, Washington was offered water from a well and he praised the quality of the town's water. Thus, from early days, the reputation of our water supply was excellent. At the turn of the century, Bird's Hill Spring Water Company was located near what became Harris Avenue and sold natural spring water.

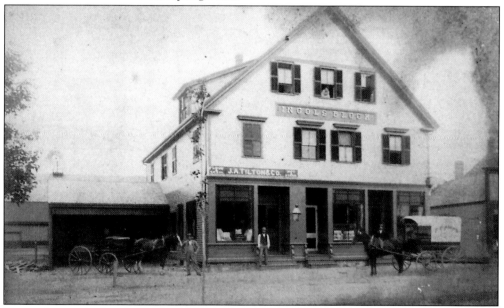

Known first as the Ingols Block and owned by a woman, this building on Chapel Street housed the J.A. Tilton Company, wholesale and retail dealers in stoves, grain, feed, hay, straw, grass seed, oil meal, cotton seed, and poultry supplies of all kinds, "at Boston prices." The building later became the Hotel Union House McKenzie, then the Hotel Nehoiden, and remains as a business building today.

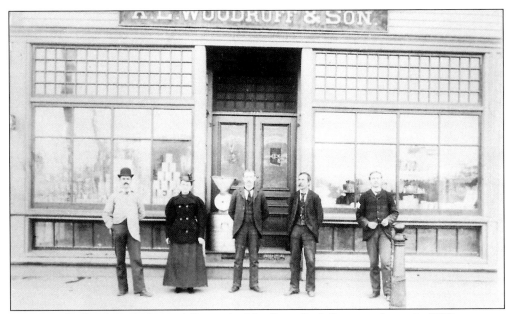

A.L. Woodruff and Son's General Store, the Needham Cash Store, is shown in 1889, one year after it was established. It was located in the May/Bourne Building on the southwest corner of Great Plain Avenue and Chestnut Street. On the floor above the market were the town hall and offices.

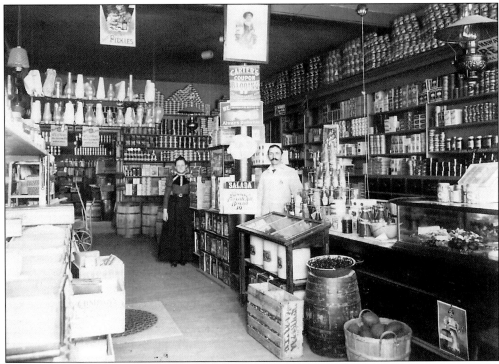

About 1900, the owner, Charles Woodruff, posed with his clerk, Miss Nellie Burkett, as the two displayed the store's wares. Moving canned goods from the pyramids on the top shelf was undoubtedly a challenge. Note the kerosene lamp globes for sale.

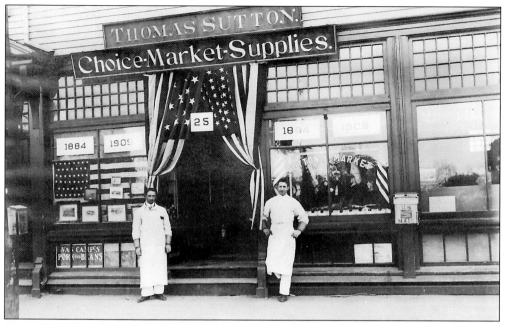

Sutton's Market, decorated in 1909 for its 25th anniversary, was established in 1884. It was located on the west corner of Great Plain Avenue and Chestnut Street in the Moseley/May/Bourne Block. The market advertised "fine butter from Montpelier, Vermont every week." By the 1930s, Sutton's Market was located on Great Plain Avenue near Maple Street. The store was in business until the 1950s.

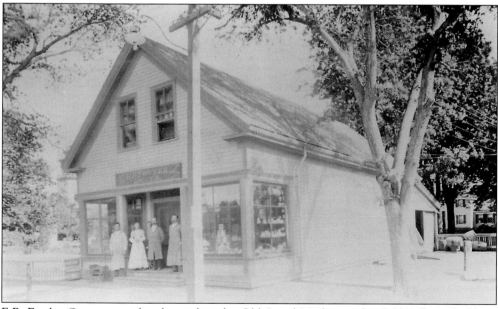

E.B. Fowler Grocery was first located in the Old Stand Market in the Odd Fellows Building. After the 1887 fire destroyed that building, Fowler moved to a separate building located at Great Plain Avenue and Chestnut Street, currently the site of Harvey's Hardware. The store housed a post office, offered free delivery to all parts of town, and sold crockery, glassware, gunpowder, window glass, hardware, paints, spectacles, and patent medicine.

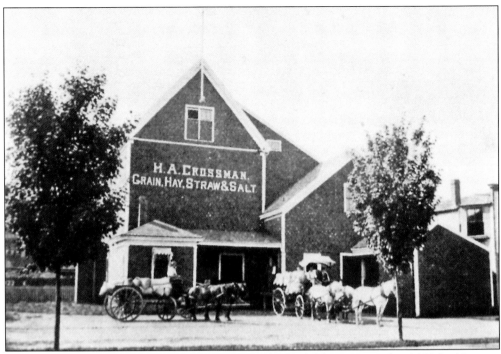

H.A. Crossman, a dealer in grain, hay, straw, and salt, did business in this 1888 building on Chapel Street across from town hall. Crossman's advertisements read: "Cow sense. Feed me with the kind of food that will make milk and I will make it. Feed me with good food that will not make milk and I cannot make it. I'll do my part if you'll do yours."

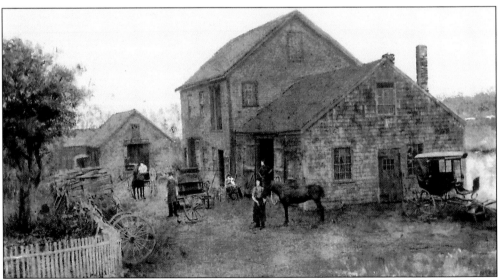

There were at least two blacksmiths' shops located on Blacksmith Pond, which was later drained for the construction of residential streets off Nehoiden Street near Rosemary Street. J.H. Fitzgerald operated his blacksmith shop in a location on Nehoiden Street near Blacksmith Pond, where hand-forged nails are found to this day. The Needham Historical Society has some of these hand-made items.

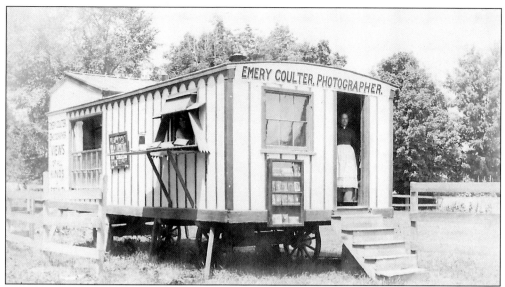

Emery Coulter, photographer, set up his studio in this wagon for the 1911 celebration of the town's 200th anniversary. Many of the pictures of the 1911 festivities originated from this mobile photograph studio.

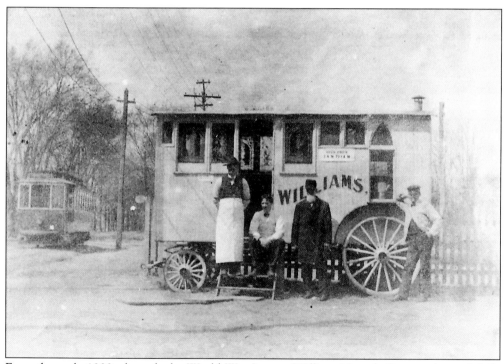

From the early 1900s through the World War I years, Williams' Lunch Cart was located daily near the Needham-Wellesley trolley-car tracks adjacent to Great Plain Avenue. Open from 7:00 am to 1:00 am, the cart served early morning coffee and was available to those on the last train at night. The cart was wheeled away and stored at the end of each workday.

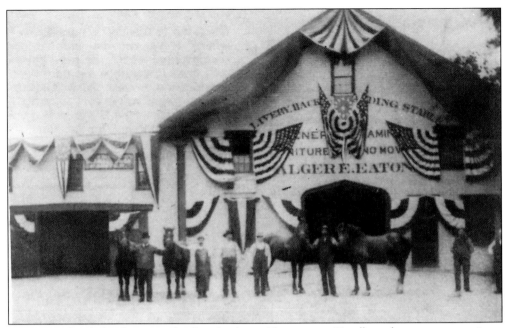

The Eaton family has been involved in the funeral business in Needham for seven generations; theirs is the oldest such family enterprise in the nation. Alger Eaton bought his uncle's livery stable in 1895. Situated next to the railroad tracks on property called Eaton Square, the livery, here decorated for the 1911 bicentennial, moved furniture, supplied funeral hearses, and rented pungs for sleigh rides and a barge to transport students. The cellar was used for embalming.

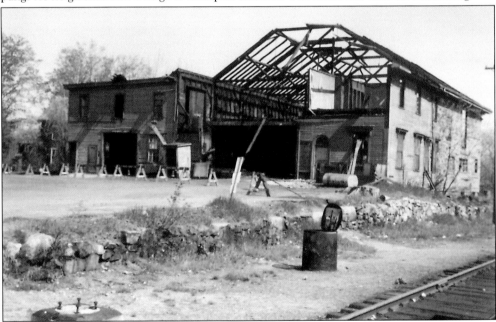

Eaton's used horses for funeral services until 1922, when the automobile put an end to the need for Eaton's stalls. The funeral business was moved to a large Colonial Revival-style house on Highland Avenue and the town bought the livery, turning it into a public works barn, which was demolished in 1961. The site is now a parking lot.

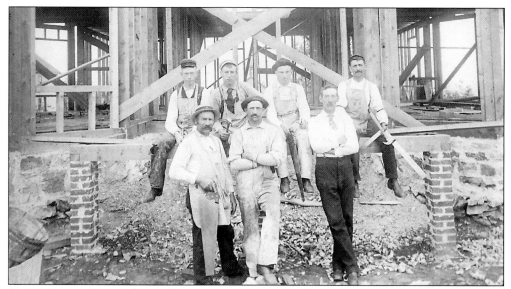

As Needham changed from a farming community to a business, industrial, and retail center, real estate development accelerated. In 1893, these carpenters put their craftsmanship to good use as they worked on a new building in Needham Heights.

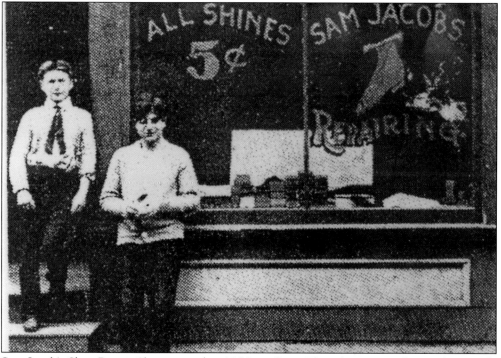

Sam Jacob's Shoe Repair Shop opened in 1906 on Great Plain Avenue on the northwest side of the railroad tracks. In 1913, Jacobs (left) moved the store to Chapel Street, and in 1927 to Chestnut Street. It was a successful shoe store featuring well-fit children's shoes and was owned by the Jacobs family until 1980. The town received a parcel of land off Central Avenue from the Jacobs family to be used as a bird sanctuary.

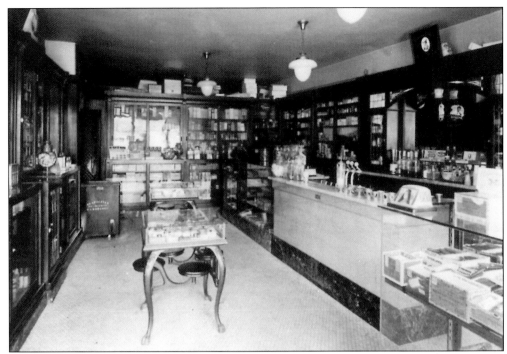

In the early 1900s, Virgil Rowe's Drug Store was located in the Low Block at the corner of Highland Avenue and West Street in Needham Heights. It contained a popular dairy and soft drink bar, and was a gathering place for young and old alike during that era almost a century ago.

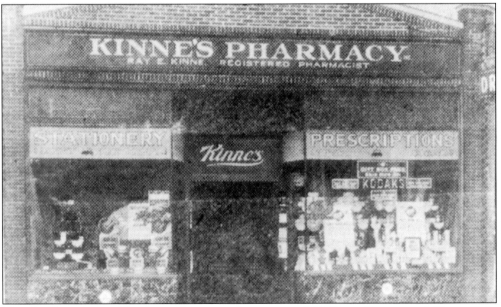

Kinne's Pharmacy in Needham Center at the corner of Dedham Avenue and Great Plain Avenue was one of more than ten locally owned drugstores in town at one period in time. Mr. Kinne entered contests with his specially decorated display windows. The pharmacy was bought by Ray Kinne in 1928 and was run by family members until 1981, becoming a local institution.

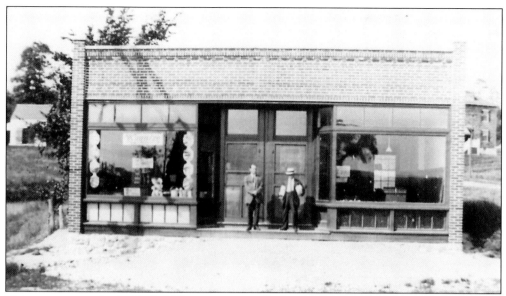

This grocery store in the Bird's Hill section originally faced Great Plain Avenue. It is seen here in a 1930s photograph, at approximately the time it became a First National Store. Subsequently, it became an independent market, the Little Red Store, and now houses Hazel's Bakery.

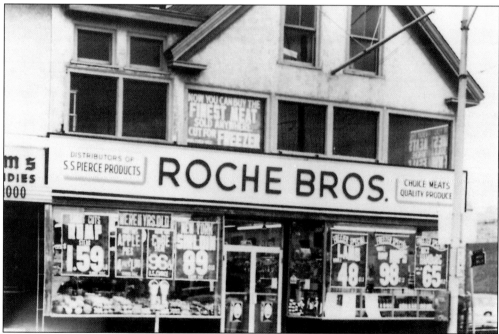

In 1959, Roche Bros. bought Crossman's Market, a longtime grocery. A town auditorium was located above Crossman's and was the meeting place for burial societies and suffrage and temperance groups. Roche Bros. moved to a new building on Chestnut Street in 1965, and Harvey's Hardware moved into the space. Eventually the market chain included ten Roche Bros. Markets and three Sudbury Farms stores, and is a "good neighbor" to community groups and causes.

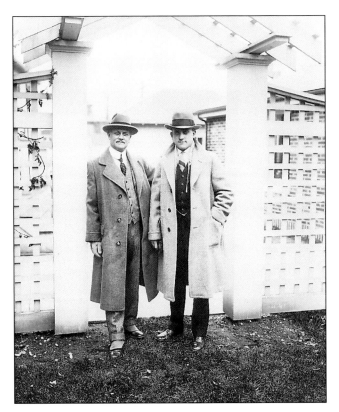

David Murdock Sr. and his son were proprietors of the Needham Paramount Theater (later Needham Cinema). Mr. Murdock Sr. was born in Scotland and died there on a return visit. He owned the house that is now the headquarters of the Needham Historical Society and named the street in front of it Glendoon Road. His first theater was on the second floor of the Moseley building in the days of silent pictures.

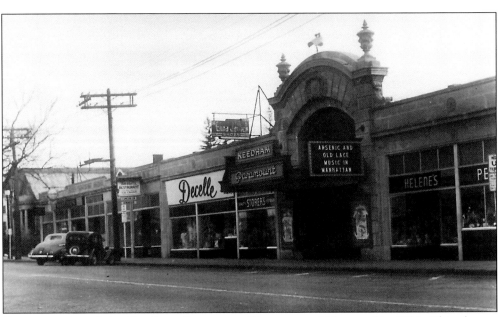

Opening night of the Needham Paramount Theater was February 11, 1926. This theater marquee from the 1940s shows that the featured film was *Arsenic and Old Lace*. After several owners, the theater eventually succumbed to the economic pressures created by large, multiple-screen theaters, and following legal entanglements was closed in 1989.

Four
Events That Shaped Our Town

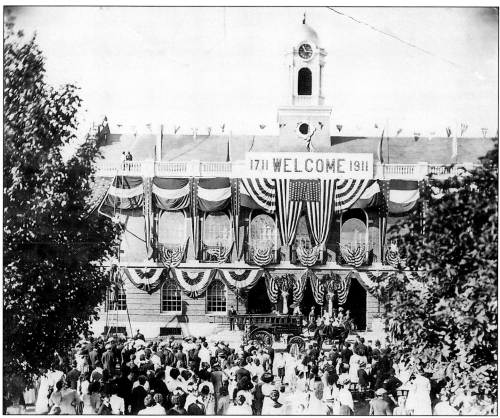

In 1911, our town hall was draped in red, white, and blue bunting for the celebration of the 200th anniversary of the incorporation of the town of Needham. Guests gathered on the town common for special programs, such as the one presented here by the fire department and their horse-drawn fire wagon, Combination No. 1. The firemen demonstrated their expertise with a hose as they sprayed the roof of the building.

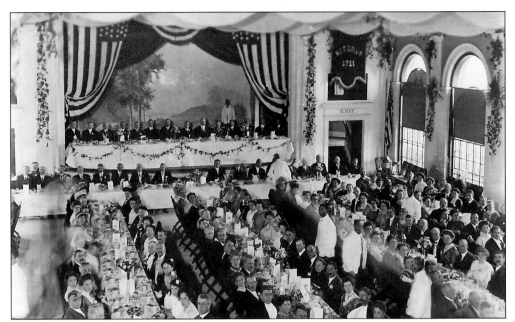

The Bicentennial Banquet was held in the second-floor auditorium of town hall in 1911. The town's dignitaries and guests were located at head tables; however, one notes the absence of distinguished ladies so seated. Cloud-like pale blue and white bunting was draped from the beams. Artificial vines and flowers adorned the room, which was used two days later for the Bicentennial Grand Ball, the town's leading social event of the year.

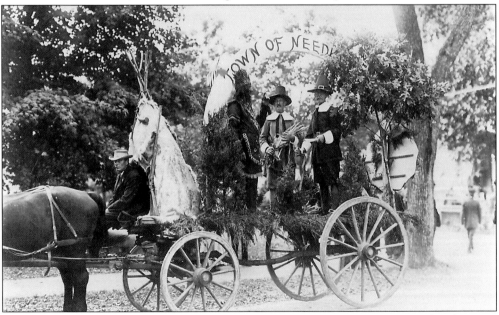

On the 1911 Needham Town Seal float, members of the Mills and Kingsbury families, two of the town's oldest and most prominent families, portrayed Nehoiden and two townsmen. Unfortunately, Nehoiden, a Massachusetts Algonquin, seems to have been dressed as a Seminole; the men of 1711 did not wear Pilgrim clothing; and the local Indians lived in wigwams, not tepees! This tableau depicted the purchase of the land that became Needham.

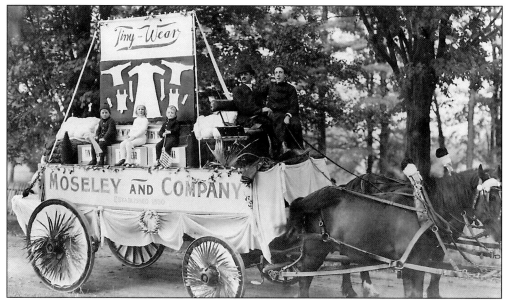

Moseley and Company, established in 1880, showed their Tiny-Wear knit products for children in their 1911 parade float. The six children on the float were the offspring of the two employees driving the wagon. Caps, leggings, sweaters, undershirts, and mittens were among the Moseley products made from skeins of yarn such as those piled on the float.

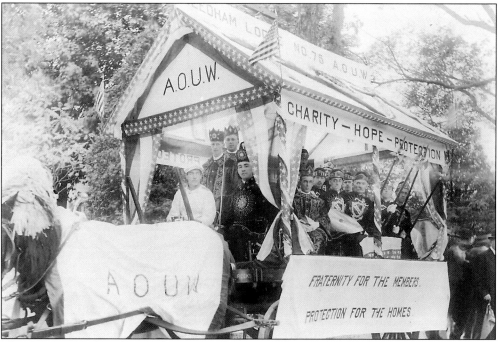

The Ancient Order of United Workmen sponsored this 1911 float. This was a benevolent fraternal insurance organization, formed in 1889 with eight members; the membership grew to two hundred by 1908. Needham men could belong to some ten similar organizations that paid benefits to survivors. With the slogan "Fraternity for the member, protection for the homes," it was the strongest organization of its kind in the country and the oldest.

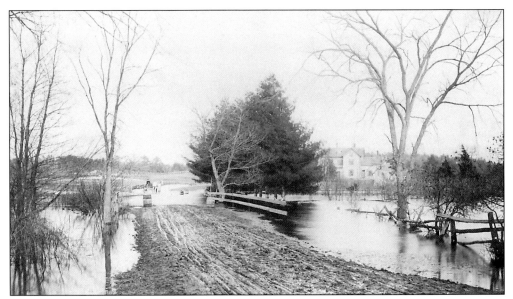

Mother Nature has taken some dramatic romps through Needham. On February 16, 1886, the Dedham Avenue bridge near South Street was flooded by the swollen Charles River after torrential rains. In the background was the home of Dr. Leach, the dentist whose office was destroyed in the 1887 fire in the Odd Fellows Building. This picture was taken from the collection of George Southworth, editor of *The Needham Chronicle*.

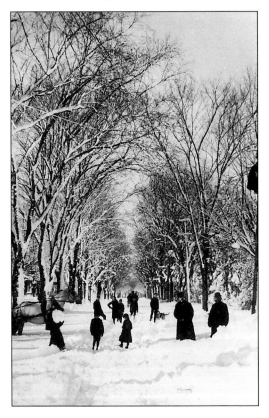

This scene shows Great Plain Avenue looking west from the railroad crossing in Needham Center on the morning after the big storm of January 31, 1898. In that era, the streets would not be plowed because residents and businesses used horse-drawn sleighs and pungs to move over the snow.

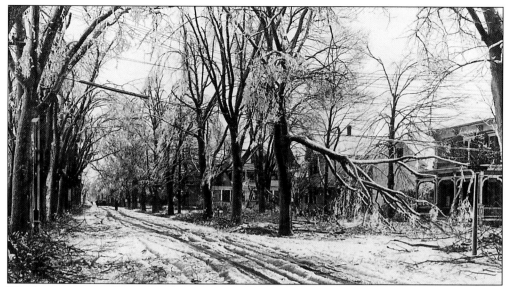
The big ice storm of 1921 resulted in the destruction of the row of handsome American elm trees that grew along the length of Great Plain Avenue. This photograph was taken at the corner of Great Plain Avenue and Linden Street. Another storm that devastated Needham's trees was the 1938 hurricane, in which over one thousand trees on town property alone were destroyed.

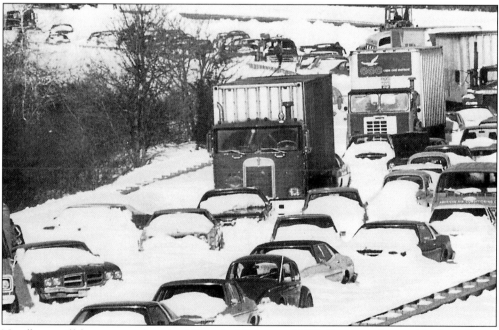
Needham will long remember the blizzard of February 1978. Because of snow blocking Route 128, more than three thousand motorists were stranded here. Merchants donated food and emergency shelters were set up in schools and churches. The governor of Massachusetts declared a state of emergency and unauthorized motorists were subject to $500 fines. Needham was completely closed down for almost one week. Total snowfall was approximately 3 feet, with drifts of 5 feet or more.

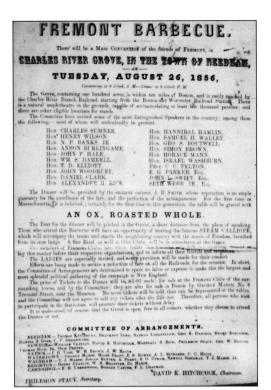

A political rally, the Fremont Barbecue, was held in 1856 at the Grove, a 100-acre site at Charles River Village, to further the cause of the New Republican Party. This demonstrated the political radicalism of Needham in that era. Present were Lincoln's future vice president Hannibal Hamlin; Senator Charles Sumner; Educator Horace Mann; Grant's future vice president Henry Wilson; and W.P. Banks, governor of Massachusetts and later a Civil War general.

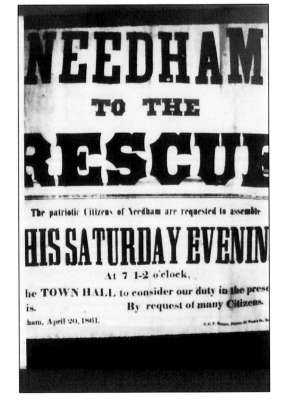

In 1861, less than ten days after the attack on Fort Sumter, Needham responded to Mr. Lincoln's call for volunteers. Ultimately, more than four hundred men were credited to Needham for service during the Civil War.

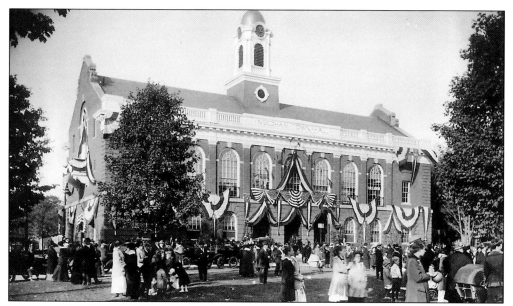

Groups of Needham residents gathered on the town common for the 1916 trade exhibition, held on October 11 and 12. Just four years after the town's bicentennial, the town hall was once again festooned with red, white, and blue for this festival, which may be seen as the forerunner of the fairs held on the town common in recent years under the sponsorship of the Needham Business Association.

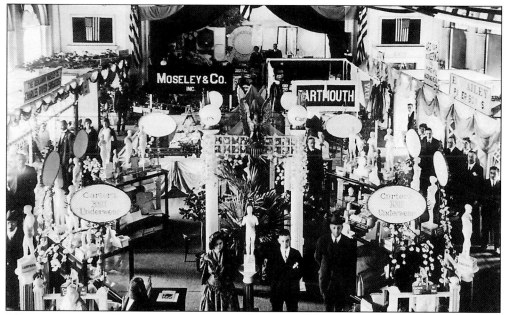

The 1916 Needham Trade Exhibition and Festival called attention to the town's many commercial activities. In addition to the underwear, sweaters, and hosiery produced by many knitting companies, Needham businesses were also making pianos, bicycles, surgical stockings, corsets, and other elastic thread products. There were several commercial florists. The large auditorium on the second floor of town hall was the display area for local wares on this occasion.

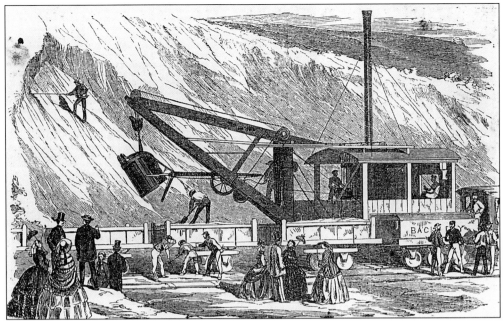

Between 1859 and the late 1870s, the area between the Charles River and the present Route 128 from Kendrick Street to Central Avenue was ravaged by the removal of its gravel and soil. For 24 hours per day, 365 days per year, this material was taken by thirty 40-car trains to fill in the 250 acres of Boston's Back Bay. Part of this Needham site is now an industrial park.

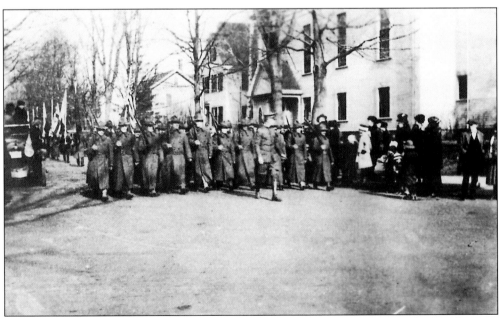

Their duty over, members of the Needham Home Guard of World War I marched in the 1918 Victory Day Parade. They had guarded local installations against possible sabotage and helped man the forts on Boston's Harbor Islands.

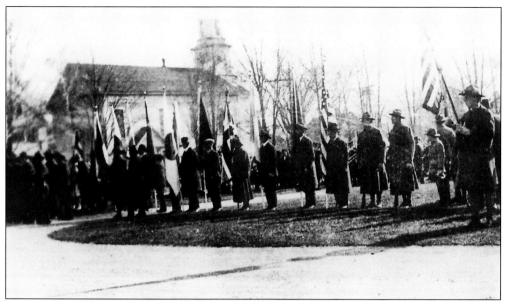

Dignitaries reviewed the World War I parade in 1918. The colors of the allies of the United States appeared on the town common, including the flags of Japan and Great Britain. In the background, the First Baptist Church stood on its original site across Highland Avenue from the town common. Many men from Needham Heights had returned to Great Britain to serve. Needham had its own company in the Yankee Division of the National Guard.

During the debate on women's suffrage, Needham groups were aligned on both sides of the issue. In 1895, the town voted down suffrage 285-184. The Needham branch of the Massachusetts Anti-Suffrage Association, with a female chairman and secretary, posted this notice for a meeting in 1915. Within five years after the ratification of the suffrage amendment, Leslie B. Cutler was elected selectman in Needham.

(POLITICAL ADVERTISEMENT)

Mr. Voter:

The Campaigners against Woman Suffrage will speak from

5.35 to 6.05 P. M., in front of T. J. Crossman's Store

—ON—

FRIDAY, OCT. 15, 1915

The Speakers on the Trip will include:
Col. John P. Irish, of California
Hon. Charles L. Underhill, of Somerville
Ex-Rep. John J. Douglass, of Boston
James M. Keyes, of Boston

AND OTHERS

Oct. 2, 1915

The party will arrive in town in autos, the tour having been outlined to cover every city, town and village in the state between September 27th and November 1st, with evening rallies in halls each night of the trip, and from ten to fourteen daylight rallies of half an hour in length on each of the six working days of each week while the tour lasts.

Col. Irish is regarded as one of the most effective orators that ever faced an audience. He began to canvass politically when he was only 18 years of age, and thus developed the gift of oratory at the very outset of his career. He has never taken part in favor of any demagogic movement. Greenbackism, free silver, socialism, woman suffrage and every like agitation have found him as their bitter and unrelenting opponent. He was the mainstay, on the stump, of the Gold Democratic protest of 1896, and carried on the fight in California almost single-handed against the woman suffrage amendments. He was the intimate friend of such men as ex-Presidents McKinley and Cleveland, Horatio Seymour, Samuel J. Tilden, and most of the public men of his own type within his time.

Messrs. Underhill and Douglass and Attorney Keyes are all strong and effective speakers.

NEEDHAM BRANCH MASS. ANTI-SUFFRAGE ASS'N,
　　　　　　　　　　　Mrs. EDWIN OWEN, Chairman,
　　　　　　　　　　　Mrs. G. W. ELLIOTT, Sec'y.

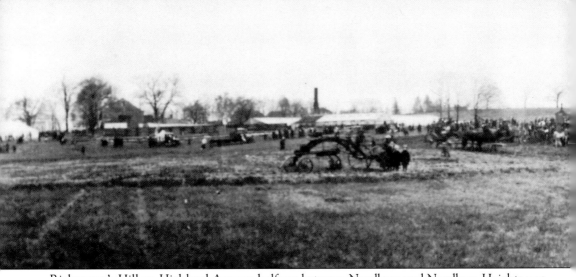

Richwagen's Hill on Highland Avenue halfway between Needham and Needham Heights was purchased for $20,000 as the site for Memorial Park. Thirteen acres of hillside were converted by more than 1,700 volunteers into an athletic complex during Memorial Park Community Day, April 19, 1921. Every available truck and team of horses in Needham was offered for the project. Alarms and bells in town called the workers to action at 7:00 am. Parades from the two

In Memoriam

RAYMOND BLADES   RALPH PATRICK
JOHN F. BOOTH   LOREN R. SMART
ROBERT BURROWS   FRANCIS W. WHITNEY
FRANCIS T. YATES

HE War is over; already, almost just a memory; as a busy people we are busy with other things, but in moments of retrospection the horror and frightfulness that our boys endured and fought against come back to us vividly.

On Community Day we shall dedicate Memorial Park to the memory of the Needham Boys who made the supreme sacrifice in the struggle for world liberty and the flag for which they fought and died will be unfurled at this time above their Memorial.

Surely no words or efforts of ours are necessary to insure the attendance of each and all of our townspeople at the services

PUBLICITY COMMITTEE FOR COMMUNITY DAY

This flyer was distributed by the Memorial Park Community Day Committee, publicizing the purpose of this volunteer project. The men, women, and children who toiled that day left a legacy to our town in the beautiful public space that has been preserved over the decades by the Trustees of Memorial Park. The area has been used for high school graduations, Fourth of July celebrations, pageants, music festivals, coasting, and sporting events.

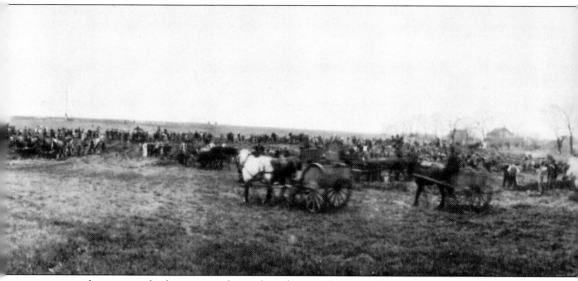

sections of town marched to join at the park and remember Needham's Minutemen. A boulder found on the land was moved to a strategic location and a bronze tablet was attached to create the World War I monument. In recent years, two community days have enlisted volunteers to remodel the park's maintenance building and to plant a large flower garden there.

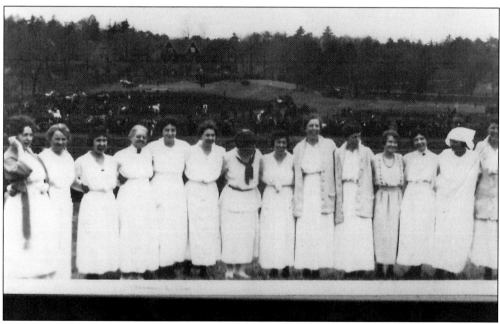

The Women's Relief Corps and Women's Auxiliary of the American Legion fed 1,700 volunteers during the Memorial Park project. The meal included 100 pots of beans, 200 loaves of bread, 200 pies, 150 pounds of frankfurters, and 175 dozen doughnuts, all donated by the women of Needham. An army field kitchen kept the food hot and demonstrated how meals were served overseas to World War I soldiers.

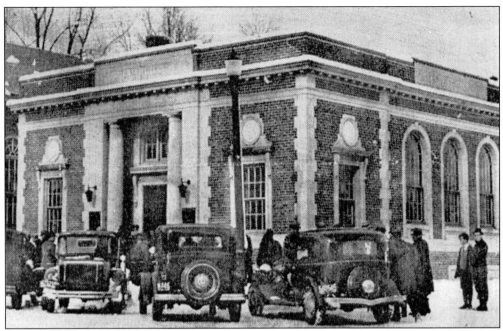

In 1934, the first machine gun bank robbery and murder in Massachusetts occurred in Needham. The Needham Trust Company was victimized by three gangsters whose precisely planned $14,000 heist was followed by a disorganized get-away. Two police officers were killed, the bank's vault keeper was injured, and a Needham firefighter was seriously wounded as bullets sprayed the bank and nearby area. The robbers were apprehended in a New York hotel and were later executed.

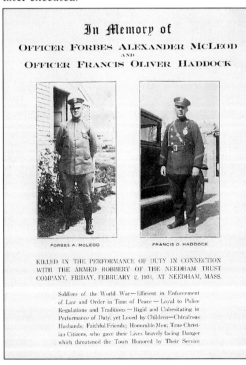

The Needham Chronicle newspaper published this supplemental page on February 16, 1934, in memory of the two Needham police officers who lost their lives in the robbery of the Needham Trust Company. The Needham Citizens' Committee raised funds to aid the families of these local heroes.

By the summer of 1940, local newspapers gave indications of a coming war. Needhamites held "Aid to The Allies" meetings and participated in the "Bundles for Britain" program. Local schoolchildren posed with the bundles that they were sending abroad, packages containing small, donated items such as soap, foodstuffs, hairpins, and toys.

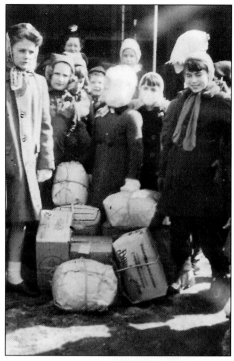

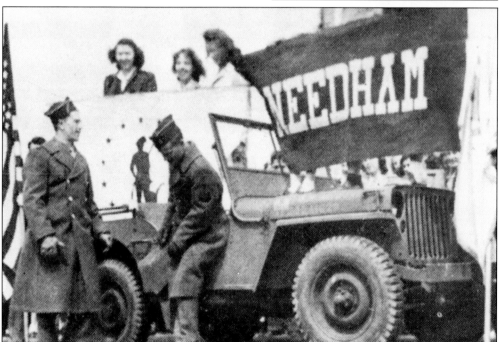

In 1943, this Jeep came to Needham High School at the end of a war bond drive. The school's goal was to raise enough funds in six weeks to purchase one Jeep; however, students collected enough for twelve vehicles, an example of how the town frequently exceeded its war goals. On one day in 1942, eight thousand people assembled on the town common subscribed to $800,000 in war bonds after they were entertained by movie star Dorothy Lamour.

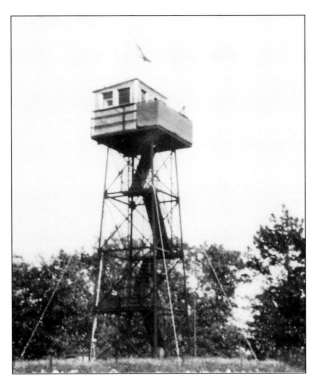

For three years during World War II, our airplane-spotting tower on Carleeta Hill was manned by the Ground Observer Corps. Volunteers watched for enemy planes. Students were given permission to cut classes for tower duty. On two occasions, Needhamites in the Army Air Corps "buzzed" the high school. On another occasion, the tower spotted a Royal Navy Air Arm training plane that crashed near Grove Street.

Needham was a Commemorative Community on the 50th anniversary of World War II. The committee collected war memorabilia, including the air raid siren from the First Baptist Church and a local defense group helmet shown here. Other projects included a memorial service for Needham's forty-eight World War II casualties and a reception attended by over five hundred people at which veterans were given certificates of appreciation by the town for their efforts.

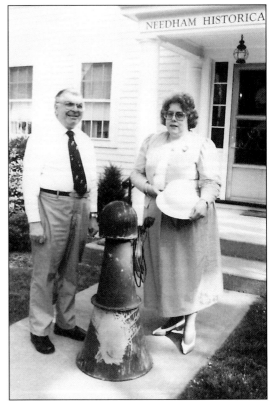

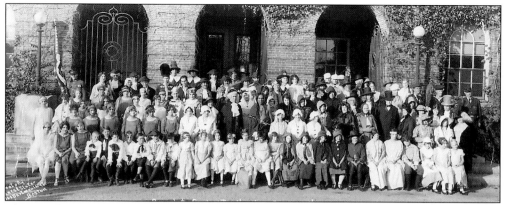

The Needham Town Pageant, held in November of 1926, featured a large cast of local residents. Portraying the important personages of our history, the characters pictured in front of town hall included our famous Indian leader Nehoiden, settlers, pilgrims, Colonial misses, government officials, Civil War and World War I soldiers, and modern 1920s girls.

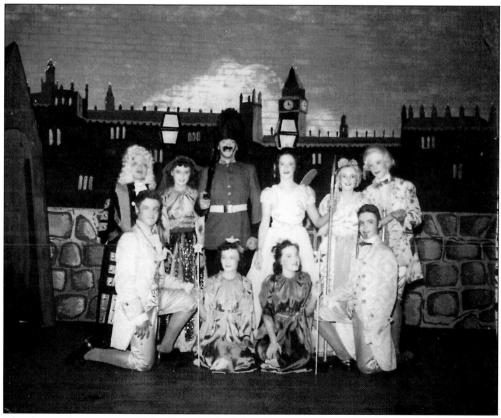

The drama department of Needham High School has staged excellent theatrical productions. In 1943, the cast of Gilbert and Sullivan's *Iolanthe* included the white-wigged Elio Semprucci; Elvira Castano Palmerio (back row, second from left), who later studied in Italy and became an opera singer and Vatican interpreter; and George Skinner (front row, far right), who became principal of Needham High School and president of the Needham Historical Society.

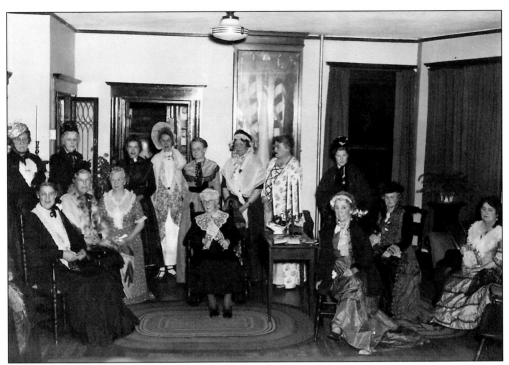

The women of the Needham Historical Society performed on October 18, 1940, in a play held at the American Legion Building at Memorial Park. The play, entitled *Memorabilia*, focused on historical items, recipes, and household chores, which were explained with sketches by costumed cast members.

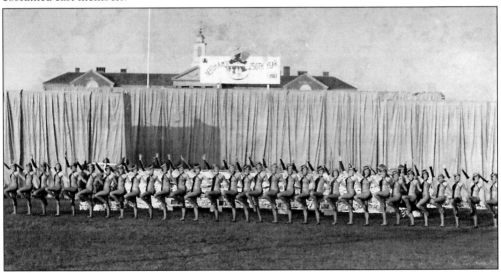

In 1961, four hundred residents participated in the town's 250th anniversary pageant, "From Red Man to Spaceman." The group gave seven performances of the twenty-episode extravaganza at Memorial Park. Eighteen thousand spectators viewed the production covering Needham's history from settlement to the space age with choreography by Paulette Harwood. Festivities included a trade fair, "shave-off" of beards grown for the occasion, placing of a time capsule, crowning of an anniversary queen, and grand celebration ball.

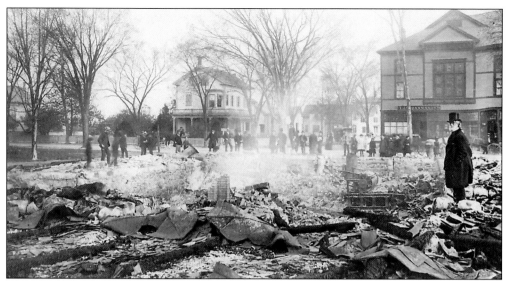

On May 12, 1887, a fire destroyed the Odd Fellows Building located on the corner of Great Plain Avenue and Chapel Street. Stores were on the ground floor, with the town's library and meeting rooms on the second. The G.A.R. post lost all of its Civil War memorabilia in the fire. At the right in the picture was dentist Dr. Elbridge Leach, whose office was in the burned structure.

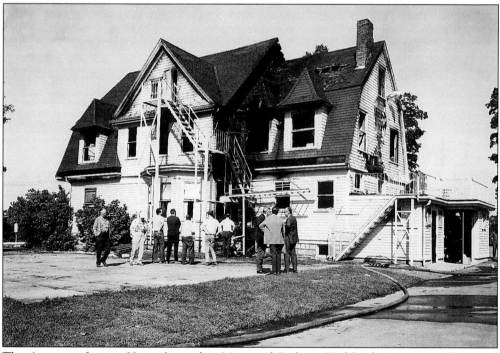

The American Legion House located at Memorial Park on Highland Avenue was destroyed by fire on September 12, 1969. The Moseley house, which had been moved to Memorial Park from Kingsbury Street, was owned by the town and leased to the American Legion. It contained elaborate wood paneling and many stained-glass windows that were part of the total loss of the structure.

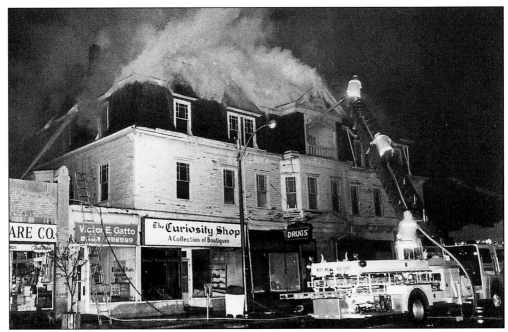

The Kingsbury Building was lost in 1980 due to improper disposal of smoking material. The building originally housed stores on the first floor, with meeting rooms and the town's major auditorium above. It was used by many local organizations before the completion of the town hall auditorium in 1902. The building was named for one of Needham's oldest families, headed by Deacon Kingsbury who owned a farm extending from the center of town to Central Avenue.

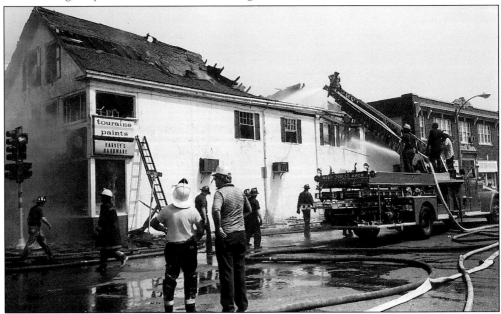

In 1977, the entire center of Needham's business district was threatened by a fire that started at Locke Lumber Company and quickly spread to Harvey's Hardware, one and one-half blocks away, due to high winds. Only heroic work by the Needham Fire Department, with mutual aid support from many neighboring towns, prevented a major town conflagration.

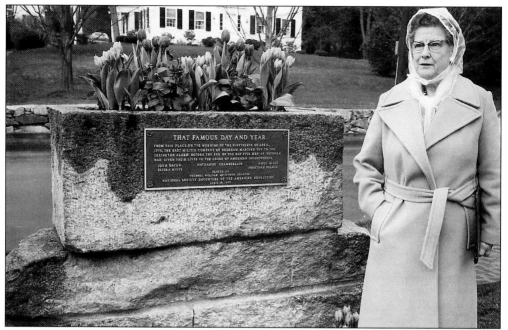

In 1979, the Colonel William McIntosh Chapter, Daughters of the American Revolution, placed a plaque on the watering trough at Townsend Green on Central Avenue at Nehoiden Street. "From this place on the morning of the nineteenth of April in 1775, the East Militia Company of Minutemen marched off to the Lexington alarm. Before the end of the day, five men of Needham had given their lives in the cause of American independence."

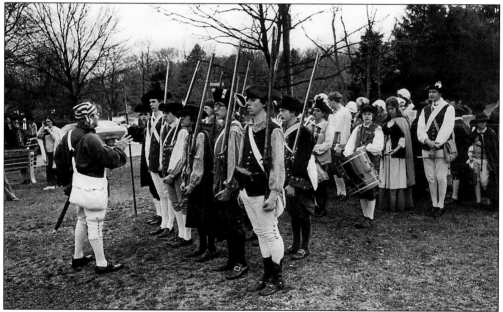

As part of our celebration of the 200th anniversary of the start of the American Revolution, Needhamites reactivated a militia unit, here adding color to the Townsend Green dedication. Needham had the second largest casualty list of any town participating in the Lexington alarm. The historical society also placed a bronze plaque on the opposite side of the watering trough.

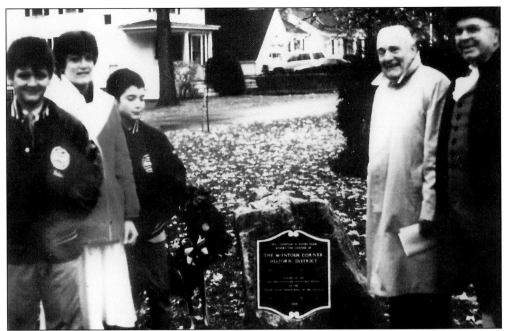

In 1991, the Needham Historical Commission dedicated the McIntosh Corner Historic District. This area at Central and Great Plain Avenues was a crossroads for travel since Indian days and became a business center. Its name honored Colonel William McIntosh, Needham Revolutionary War leader. Members of the McIntosh family joined "Colonel William" at right, portrayed by Henry Hicks.

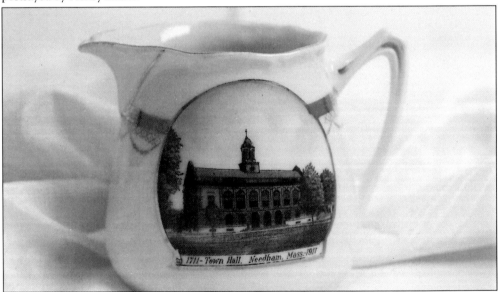

The Needham Historical Society recently acquired this china creamer found by a New Hampshire antique dealer. The creamer was a souvenir of the town's great 200th anniversary festival in 1911. The T.J. Crossman General Store commissioned the production of this china from the Altenburg Company in Germany. Each piece featured a town building; this example depicts the town hall.

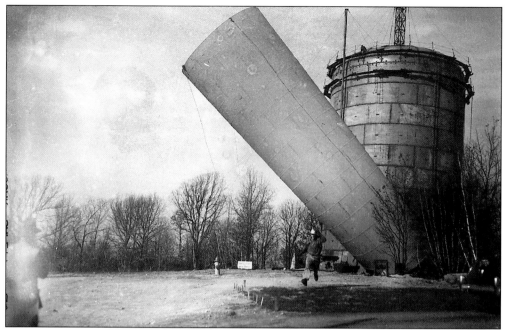

A sixty-year-old water storage tank on Ryan's Hill in the Carleeta Park section was replaced in 1950. The new $75,000 standpipe with a capacity of more than one million gallons was erected to replace the old standpipe, which fell only after a three-hour struggle. This picture was printed in newspapers all over the country, probably due to interest in whether the workman in the foreground had successfully run out of harm's way. (He had.)

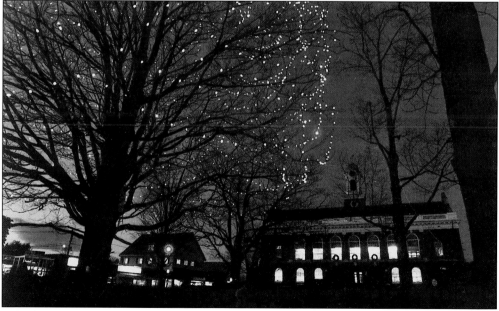

A highlight of the December holiday season in Needham is the "Blue Tree" that is lighted on the Sunday after Thanksgiving and decorated in bulbs of the "town color." The tradition has been carried out since 1954 when the Needham Board of Trade first proposed the idea. In recent years the Needham Business Association has been responsible for this unique event.

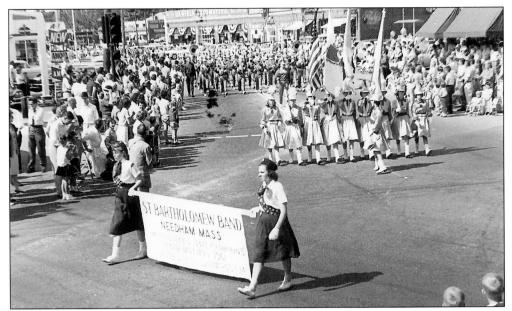

The Fourth of July in Needham is the quintessential hometown patriotic holiday celebration. Sponsored for almost fifty years by the Needham Exchange Club, the Independence Day celebration in our town features vestiges of times past, including a concert, road race, and barbecue. A highlight is a parade viewed by thousands of people. The St. Bartholomew Band, 1961 American Legion State Champion, is typical of the bands and other units that have marched in the procession.

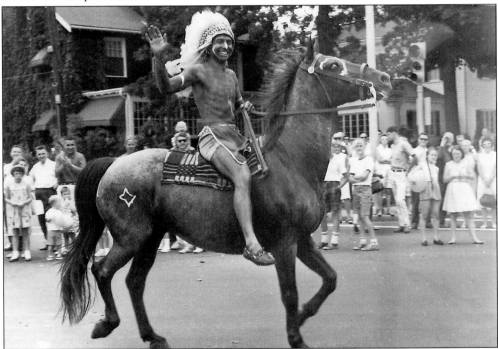

Local businessman Fred Muzi has been a feature of the Independence Day parade for many years. He greets the crowd from horseback.

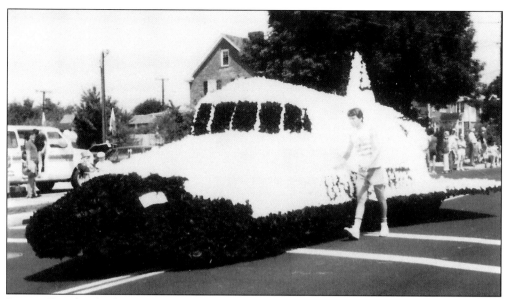

In one Fourth of July parade, NASA and the space program were highlighted by this self-propelled version of the space shuttle, a monumental design in crepe paper stuffing and chicken-wire construction.

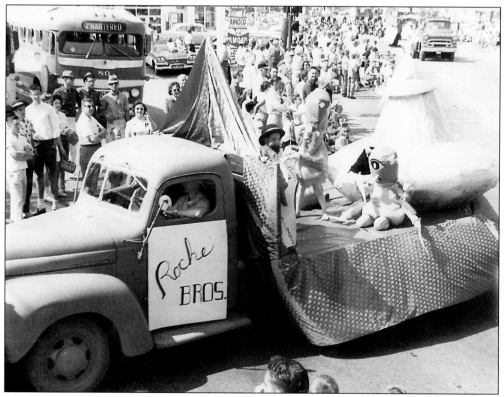

Another frequent presence in the Fourth of July parade has been Roche Bros. Supermarkets, long a generous sponsor of local organizations and activities. In this entry, a spaceship brought little aliens to our town, where they were met by a young bearded settler.

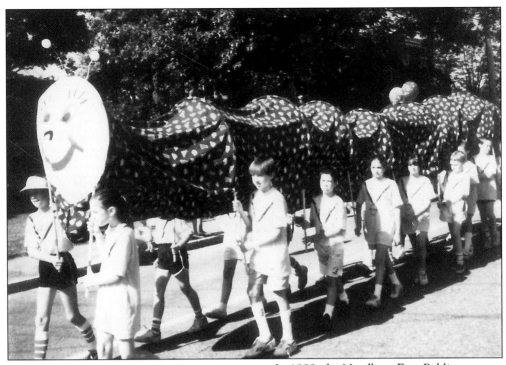

In 1988, the Needham Free Public Library, in celebration of their centennial, brought Centi-Pete to the parade. In that Centennial Olympics year, the animators of Centi-Pete had "Olympic Medals" on their costumes and declared on their sign: "Every Reader Wins." Sponsored by the Friends of the Library, the entry won the Wyeth Award for originality of design, one of many trophies presented after each parade by the Needham Exchange Club.

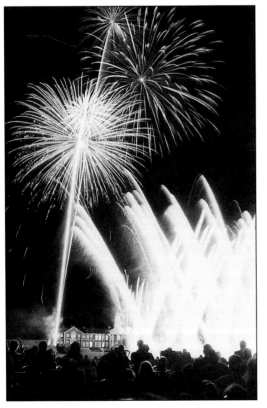

Old-fashioned fireworks displays are part of Needham's Independence Day celebration. The summer sky glows and the ground shakes with their splendid bursts. Held on July 3 at Memorial Field, the fireworks set the mood for the next day's festivities of parade, flea market, foot race, swim meet, and ballgames. Traditions are important on this day and our children are learning these by participation in our outstanding celebration of this most glorious national holiday.

Five
Our Architectural History

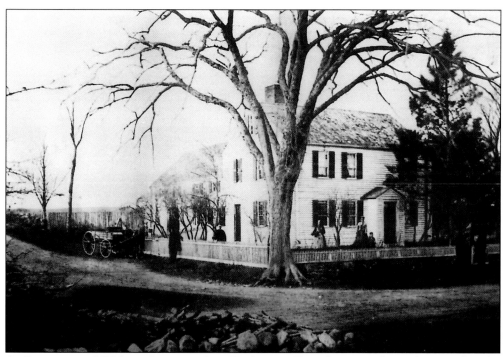

At Rosemary and Webster Streets is the 1779 house of Jonathan Kingsbury who served in the American Revolution. His property consisted of 20 acres around the house and 87 acres across Webster Street. Paul Richwagen, florist, lived there for thirty-four years. The front door of the house originally faced Webster Street, as shown here, and was later replaced by a chimney when the door was moved to the Rosemary Street side.

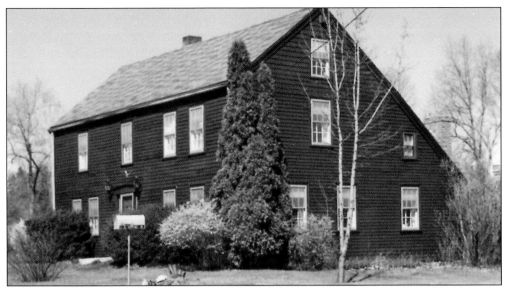

The Robert Fuller House, Needham's oldest existing residence, an early Colonial saltbox, was built on Burrell Lane in 1707. Fuller was a signer of the 1710 petition that led to Needham's separation from Dedham. The residence housed itinerant ministers and was used for church and school. Fuller moved the house 500 feet down the lane in 1735 for his son, Lieutenant Robert Fuller Jr., and built himself another home on the old site.

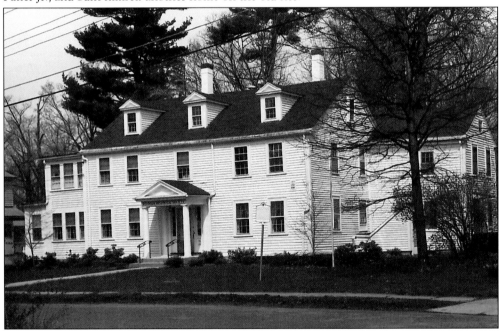

Headquarters of the Needham Historical Society since 1949, the Kingsbury-Whitaker House (c.1710–1840) on Glendoon Road stands on land that was part of a 92-acre farm owned in the early 1700s by Deacon Kingsbury, signer of the Dedham Farmers' Petition and our first town clerk. Edgar Whitaker, Boston merchant and director of the company that brought the railroad to Needham, used the frame of the Kingsbury house for the construction of this building in 1840.

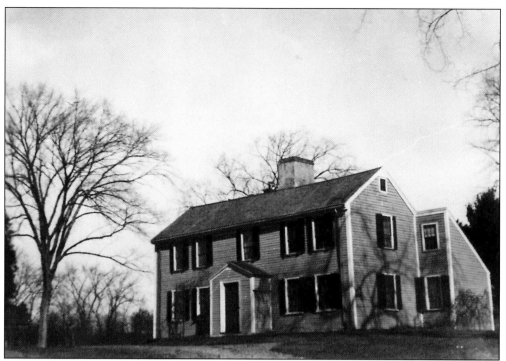

Built in 1754 by Amos Fuller, this house and its nineteenth-century barn are reminders of Needham's rural past. The barn is the oldest barn extant in town. James McCracken, owner in 1922, named the property "Hearthstone Farm" and gave a section of the land for Girl Scout Camp Malcolm in memory of his son. The McCrackens presented 15 acres of their property to Needham for conservation land in 1984.

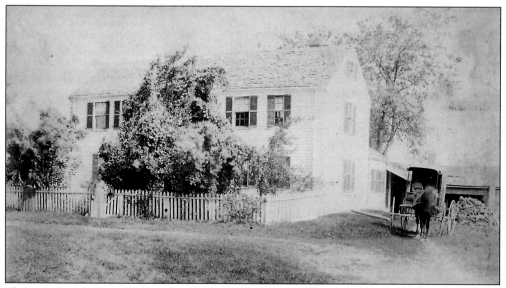

This was the Mackintosh Homestead, bought by Colonel William McIntosh (who changed the spelling of his name) in 1764 when it probably was not a new house. It had a sloping roof at the rear before being remodeled in the early 1820s. This picture was taken in 1884. The house was demolished c. 1889 and a new one was built on the site by Mackintosh family members.

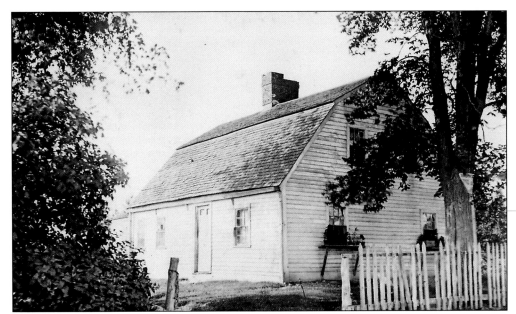

Photographed c. 1890, this gambrel-roofed cottage in Charles River Village was known as the Paine-Mills house. Ephraim Paine, the town sealer of leather from 1757 to 1791, lived here c. 1770. Paine, a French and Indian War veteran, was chosen by the selectmen to provide for families of deceased Continental Army soldiers in an early form of welfare. The house was razed in 1971.

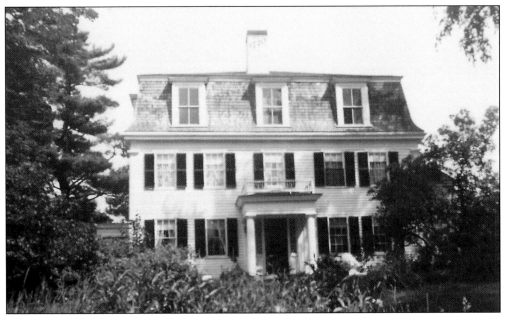

At Central Avenue and Nehoiden Street is the house built in 1720 for our first resident minister, the Reverend Mr. Jonathan Townsend. The East Militia Company left from this house to answer the Lexington alarm in 1775. The militia kept supplies in the house during the Revolutionary War. Until 1821, it housed the first three ministers of the town, and, later, historian George Kuhn Clarke. The mansard roof was added in the 1850s.

Built c. 1776 on land acquired for 95 bushels of corn, the Joshua Lewis house was purchased in 1874 by Denys Zirngiebel, developer of the giant Swiss pansy and modern carnation. This house was later the home of N.C. Wyeth, his grandson. Wyeth used the house in his painting *Christmas Morning*, now owned by the Needham Historical Society. The elderly gentleman in the painting was his grandfather Zirngiebel and the boy his brother Stimson.

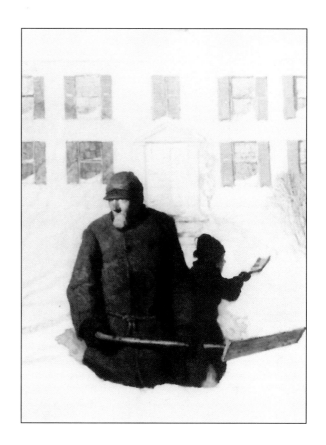

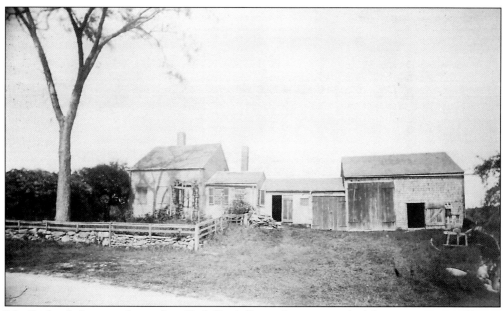

The Richards farm was located on High Rock Street. It was typical of the interconnected house and barn found in the area in the mid- to late nineteenth century.

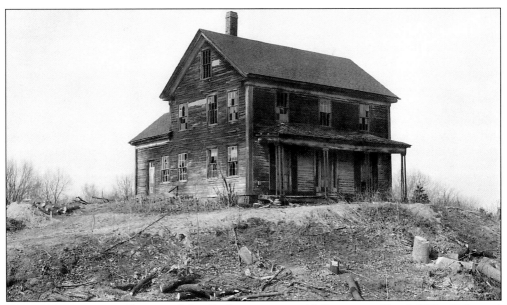

This old house, originally part of the Cook property, c. 1942 sat atop North Hill off Central Avenue on land purchased by the federal government, which used the area for a Nike missile control site. The structure was an abandoned relic of an old farm and made way for the most modern military defense system installation of the time.

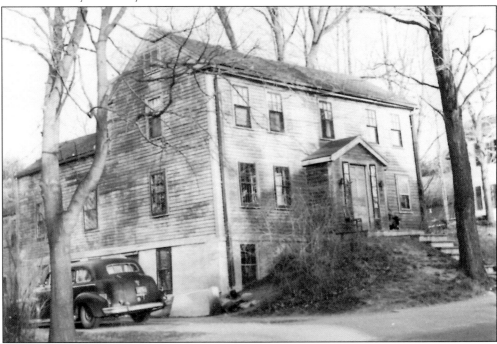

Luther Morse, blacksmith, built this Colonial home on Nehoiden Street in 1832. His shop was on a small pond on the property. In 1925 the site was purchased by Sidney and Elizabeth Stewart, antique dealers. Mr. Stewart was president of the Needham Historical Society from the late 1940s into the 1960s. In a basement shop on the premises, Stewart had a furniture restoring business and was consulted by museums for his expertise.

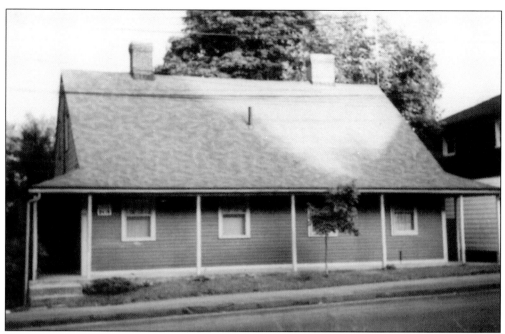

Built in 1834, the Tyler-Pettee House on Central Avenue is a simple story-and-a-half frame dwelling. Pettee operated a cobbler's shop near his home, which was built as a double house with two kitchen fireplaces in the cellar. Typical of the mill workers' houses of New England industrial areas and located near the sites of former textile mills on the Charles River, this is the only mill house remaining in Needham.

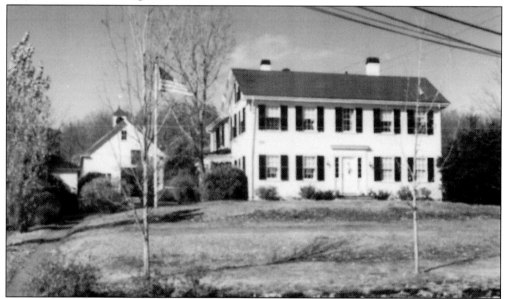

The Davis Mills house, now North Hill Farm, was built 1834–35 in the Late Colonial style. It overlooks the original center of town, now Townsend Green, which is cared for by the Richard Toran family, the current residents of the house. Standing at his door, Mills could see the second meetinghouse, post office, brick schoolhouse, militia field, minister's house, and road to the burying ground. Mills, a butcher, operated a slaughterhouse on the premises.

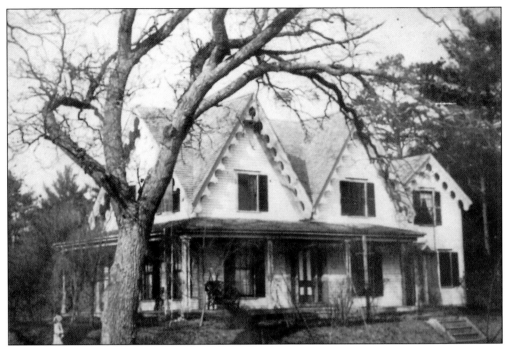

This Carpenter's Gothic-style home on Garden Street, built in 1855, sits on two terraces above its sunken front lawn. At the left of the house, a road once led down to spring-fed property at the rear. The land on which it stands was once part of the large Deacon Timothy Kingsbury farm. The house was owned by Susie Gay Whitney, president of the Needham Historical Society.

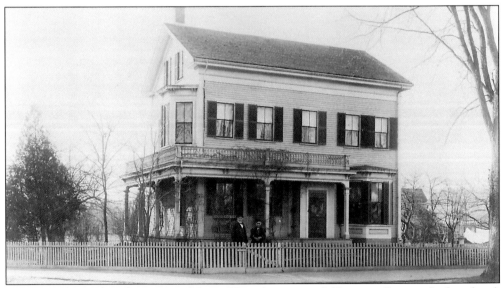

This home located at the corner of Great Plain Avenue and Chestnut Street, which it faced, was the residence of Mr. and Mrs. Edmund Broadley Fowler. The house was razed and a business block was erected on that site extending east along Great Plain Avenue. This corner location later became T.J. Crossman's store, then Roche Bros. Market, and today is Harvey's Hardware, with offices on the second floor.

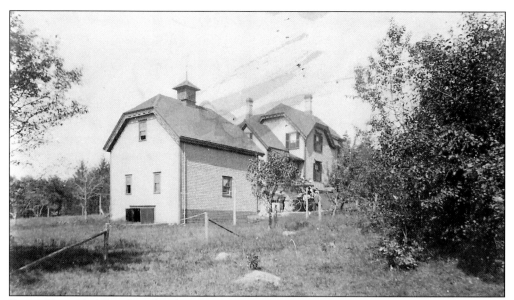

Denys Zirngiebel lived in this house on South Street near his Greendale Greenhouses. It is believed that his grandson, artist N.C. Wyeth, used this house as inspiration for his illustration of the Admiral Benbow Inn in the background of a picture of Old Blind Pew for Robert Louis Stevenson's *Treasure Island*.

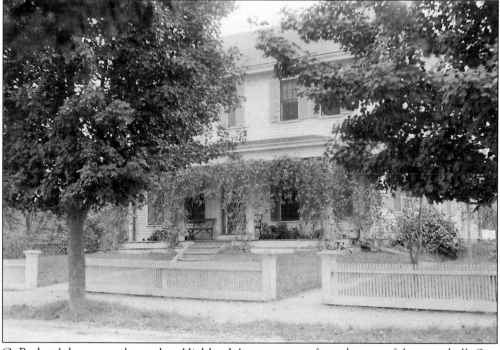

G. Burkett's house was located on Highland Avenue across from the rear of the town hall. One of the lovely houses that once were located on two sides of the town common area, it was taken down and replaced by the Bourne Piano Factory, which ceased production in 1935. The site was subsequently the home of McGregor Instrument Company, a W.T. Grant store, and a Bed and Bath store, and now houses medical offices.

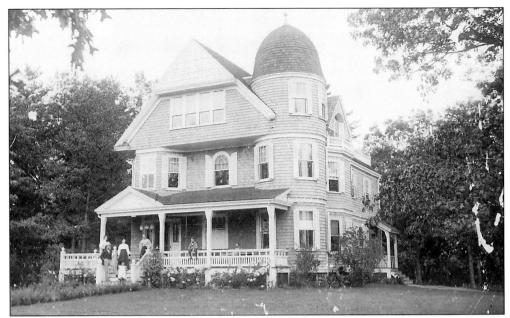

The Berthold house, located at the corner of Webster Street and Harris Avenue, was an elegant example of the many Late Victorian-style homes built in Needham in the late nineteenth century. Many wealthy Boston residents built similar large homes in Needham, where they summered; year-round Needham residents built such houses as well, a sign of increasing prosperity in the community.

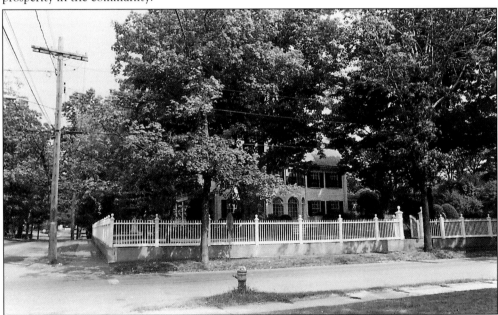

Forty Grant Street, home of James Henry Powers, foreign editor of the *Boston Globe*, was built in 1905 for $5,000. Powers was one of the few editors whose columns President Franklin D. Roosevelt admired. During World War II, Powers acted as an advisor to intelligence agencies of the Free French, Great Britain, and the United States, whose operatives visited this house as "businessmen."

Spanning the Charles River between Needham and Newton, Echo Bridge was completed in 1876. It carried the Sudbury River aqueduct into a brick tunnel leading to Boston. Standing below the 70-foot-tall central arch, one can hear many echoes. A footbridge on top leads to Hemlock Gorge, site of Indian caves. The area is now a Metropolitan District Commission reservation and is under restoration.

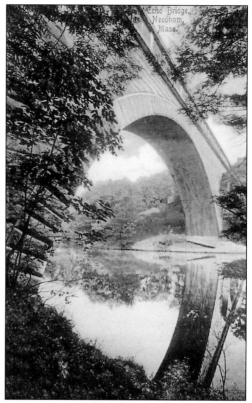

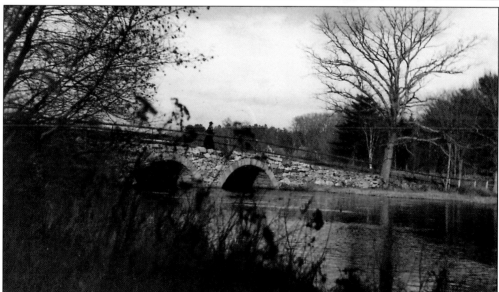

Although the present stone bridge was constructed in 1847, the Charles River was spanned here early in the eighteenth century at this western terminus of Central Avenue. This bridge was kept in repair by the Fisher family, from whom it gets its present name. Central Avenue was originally called Fisher's Meeting Road, and connected that family's farm with the meetinghouse on Nehoiden Street. The area was an early Indian river crossing.

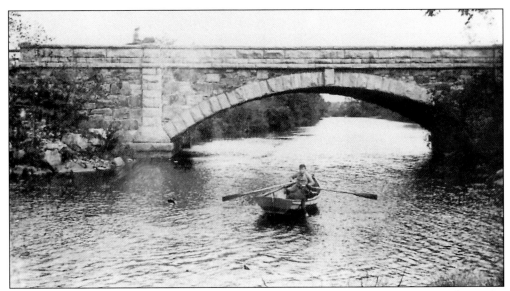

Site of one of the earliest bridges connecting Needham to its mother town of Dedham, the present Lyon's Bridge at Greendale Avenue was built in 1877. It acquired its present name from the Lyon family that owned much of the adjoining property. A famous son of the family, Dr. Israel Whitney Lyon, developed commercial tooth powder. The rower is N.C. Wyeth.

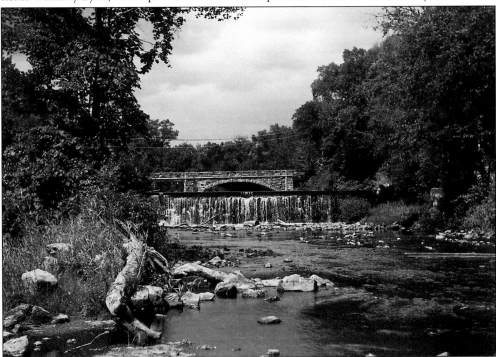

In 1675, a dam was located on South Street at the Charles River for Fisher's gristmill. Now Cochran Dam Bridge, it was at various times the site of two paper mills, a nail factory, two textile mills, and later an automobile tire factory. Below the bridge and dam is a kayak raceway, usable when the river is high. This area was a major early Indian fishing site. Nearby is Red Wing Bay, once a popular canoe rental location.

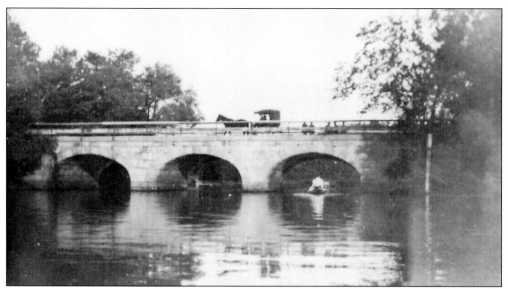

Located at the eastern terminus of Highland Avenue, the Highland Avenue Bridge was the last of the nine bridges built (1875) across the Charles River into Needham. This construction was necessitated by the shift of the center of town to the Great Plain with the building of the railroad. The area was the site of a canoe rental boathouse. Because of the development of the Needham Industrial Park, this is probably the busiest of our bridges.

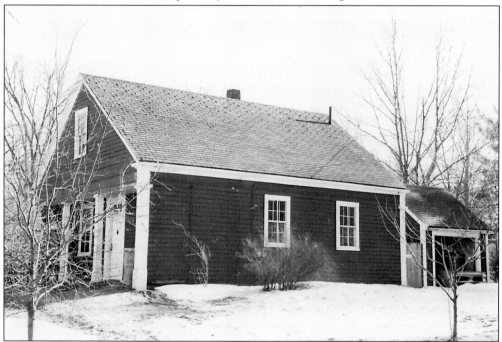

Needham's oldest remaining school building at 278 Central Avenue is today a private residence. Called the Little Red Schoolhouse, it was built in 1842 at a cost of $600 to replace the nearby 1807 East District School, which had been "unfit for some time." Sold at public auction in 1869, having been declared outdated and overcrowded, it was replaced by what was to become the first Eliot School.

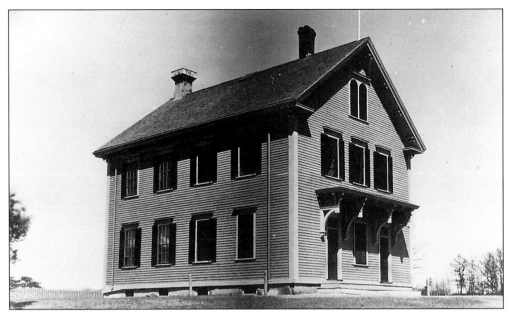

The original Harris School, built in 1855, was called the Plains School. Located first at Great Plain Avenue and Manning Street, it was moved in 1872 to the Greendale District and located at Great Plain Avenue and Green Street, a section known as Pudding Point. The building originally had two rooms, one up and one down. Demolished in 1938, the lumber was donated to the Boy Scouts for a camp in High Rock Woods.

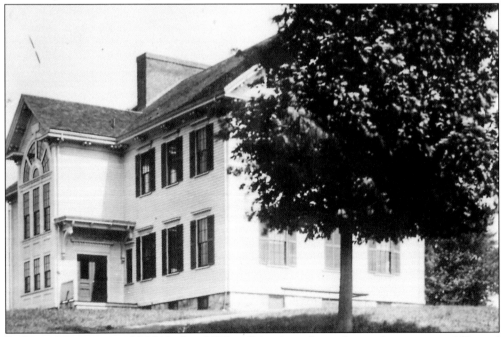

Built in 1869 at a cost of $6,000, the old Eliot School was located near the junction of Central Avenue and St. Mary's Street. It was known first as the Upper Falls School and then as the East School. The facility was named in 1886 in memory of the Reverend John Eliot, who was an apostle to the local Indian tribes in the late 1600s.

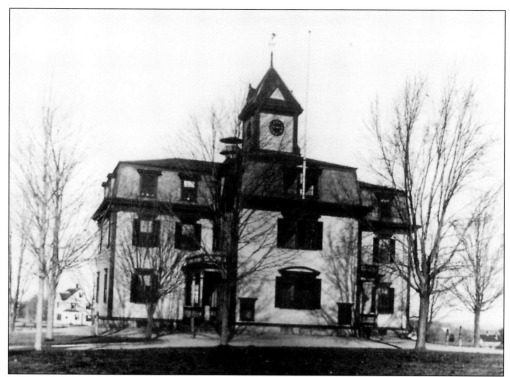

In 1869 the town spent $6,000 on a new school in Highlandville, built on land purchased from Jonathan Avery, a prominent businessman and father-in-law of William Carter, for whom a school was named directly across the street. The three-story Avery contained rooms heated by individual stoves. It was enlarged in 1885 and steam heat added, using monies from the Wellesley settlement over the division of Needham.

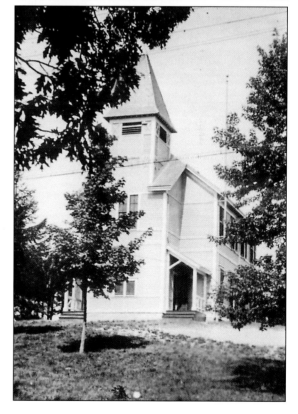

Located in Charles River Village, the Parker School, built in 1876 at a cost of $4,593, resembled a church. Its bell was eventually used at the old Needham Heights Fire Station and now sits in front of the historical society headquarters. Demolished in 1941, the school was named for Jonathan Parker, who literally left his plough in the field to answer the Lexington alarm of April 1775, which cost him his life.

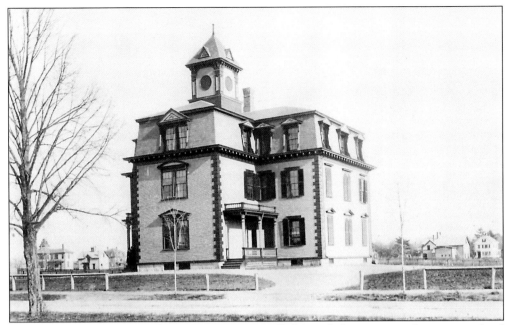

The Kimball School, opened in 1871, was a centrally located elementary and grammar school on the corner of Chestnut and School Streets, the site of the present police and fire stations. It was named for the Reverend Daniel Kimball, who operated a private academy at Marked Tree Road and Great Plain Avenue.

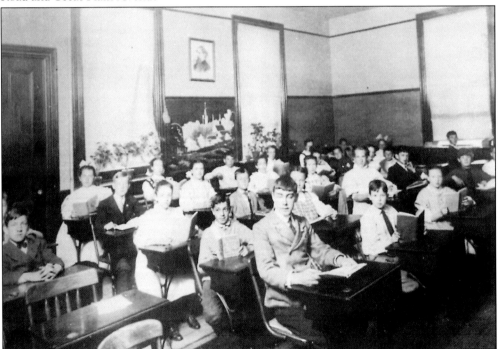

Before the 1898 construction of the Emery Grover building, Kimball Grammar School also housed the high school on the upper floor. This class included students between the ages of eleven and fourteen.

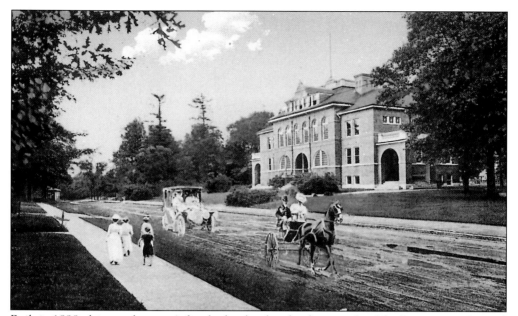

Built in 1898, this was the town's first high school and only example of the Renaissance Revival style. It was built halfway between the two sections of town on a site donated by knitting company owner John Moseley. Named for Judge Emery Grover, a twenty-two-year member of the school committee, the building has been the office of the school administration since 1930 and is listed on the National Register of Historic Places.

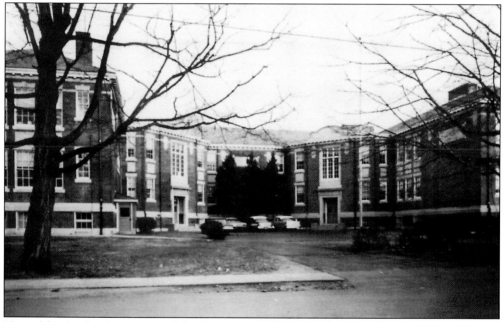

Named for the first historian and third minister of the town who served from 1792 to 1821, the Stephen Palmer School was built in 1914 near the town's center. When the Kimball School was demolished in 1929, a wing was added to this building to accommodate the district's students. The Stephen Palmer School was closed in 1975 and was remodeled into residential apartments. The Needham Senior Citizens Center is also located in this building.

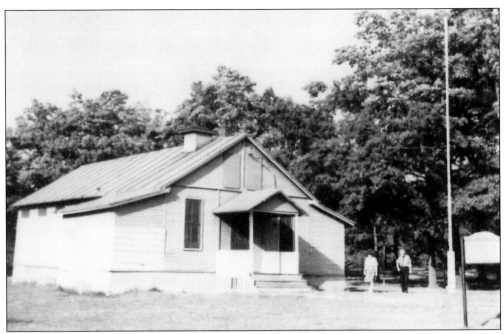

With the development of industry on the Newton side of the Charles River, the area next to the current Route 128 became attractive for working family housing. An ethnically diverse neighborhood (called Riverside) developed and it had its own school. The Riverside School was put in and out of use depending on the school population.

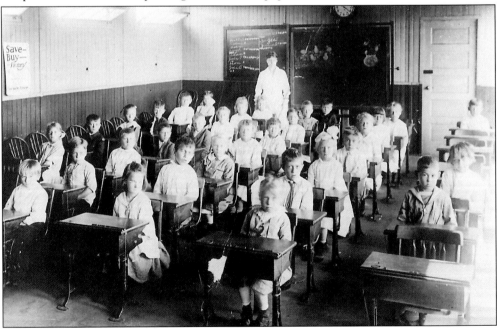

In 1918 these students attended Riverside School, a two-room building on the edge of Needham Heights. This was a large primary class, including grades 1 to 3. Note the World War I Victory Bond Drive poster on the wall. The school was condemned in 1944 and then used as a park and recreation department storage facility before being razed.

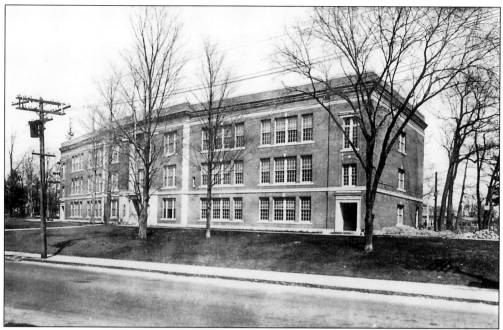

With rapid population growth in Needham after World War I, the 1898 high school building proved inadequate. The town needed a modern facility with a gym and science rooms. The Highland Avenue School was located next to the old high school. This new building also became inadequate for a high school; it served as a junior high and finally an elementary school before it was razed and the site used for a condominium development.

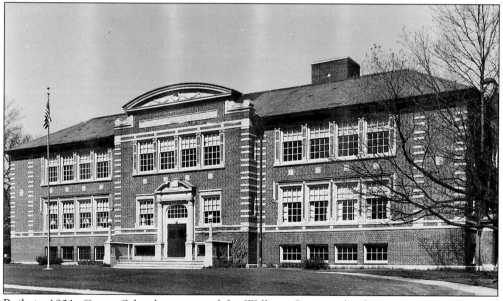

Built in 1921, Carter School was named for William Carter, school committee member and founder of the Carter knitting mills. An English immigrant in the 1850s, Carter's business success stemmed from his reputation for hard work and integrity. The building was returned to the town by the school committee in 1981 and an apartment complex was built on the site following demolition of the school.

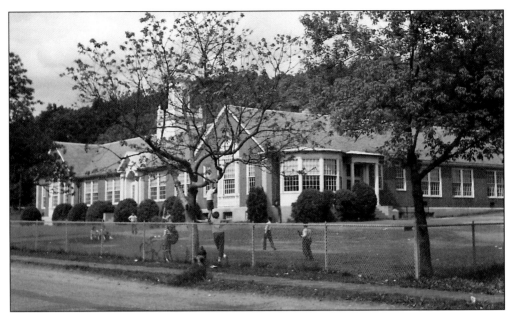

The "new" Harris School was built in 1930 on Beaufort Avenue on land purchased from the Broadley Farm. Enlarged in 1938, it was razed in 1982 and the school lot was made into a playground park named for teacher/principal Rebecca H. Perry. The Harris Schools were named for John Morton Harris, civil engineer, member of the school committee, and representative to the General Court.

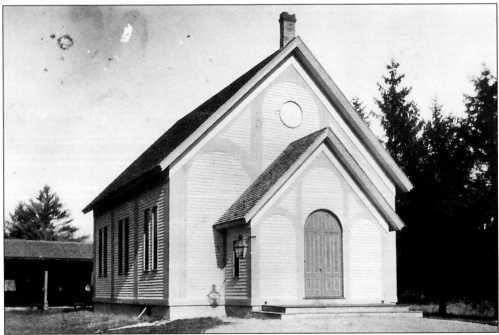

Chapel Street in the town's center was named for the Orthodox Congregational chapel that stood at the far end of a 35-foot right-of-way to Great Plain Avenue. Dedicated in 1859 and built at a cost of $1,500, this chapel was the predecessor of the Evangelical Congregational church. Sold at auction in 1890, it was taken down c. 1928.

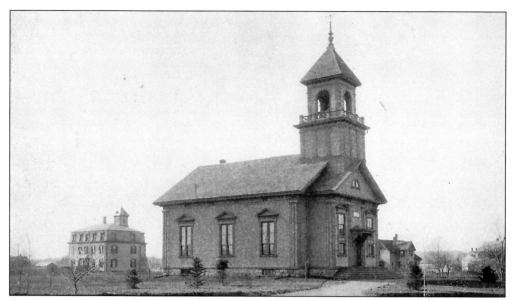

As old as the town itself, the First Parish Church, originally Congregational and now Unitarian Universalist, has had three buildings and two locations. The present Dedham Avenue/Great Plain Avenue building is the 1836 church from lower Nehoiden Street, moved in 1879 to the present location. This reflects the removal of the town's center up onto the Great Plain. A bell cast by Paul Revere hangs in the church. In the background is the Kimball Grammar School.

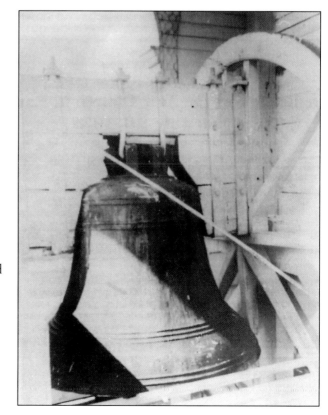

In 1811, for the town's centennial, the First Parish Church purchased this 960-pound Paul Revere bell for $407.61 and installed it in the tower of their second church, built in 1774. The bell was also used in the third church structure built on the site in 1836. In 1879 the church and the bell were moved to their present location at Great Plain and Dedham Avenues.

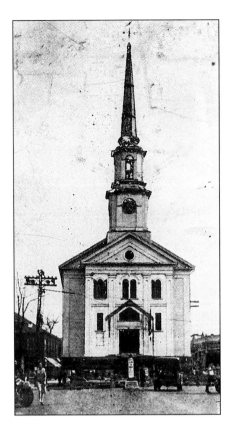

Although there was a Baptist church here in 1780, the present congregation dates from 1856. Named the "First Baptist Church in Needham" in 1888, it was located at Great Plain and Highland Avenues, site of the present Fleet Bank. In 1928, the church was moved east up Great Plain Avenue. Its pastor, the Reverend Samuel Smith, wrote the words to "My country, 'Tis of Thee." The church housed our World War II air raid siren.

The Needham circuit of the Methodist Episcopal church dates back to the 1790s, but the present Methodist presence reflects the coming of Wesleyan English knitters to Highlandville. In 1867 the church was established. Generous donations of land and money from William Carter created the church pictured here in the 1870s. In 1950, ground was broken for the present Carter Memorial United Methodist Church.

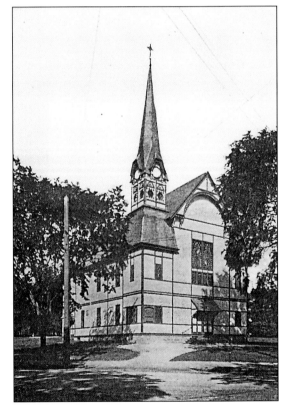

St. Joseph's Roman Catholic Church was established as a mission in 1890 with the purchase of the former Congregational chapel. In 1891, the wooden, first St. Joseph's was built at the corner of Highland Avenue and May Street and was destroyed by fire in 1913.

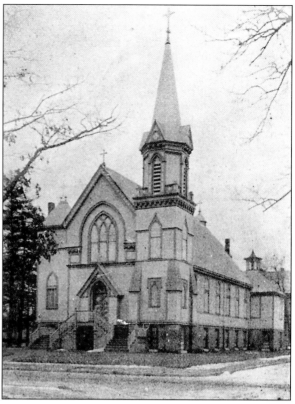

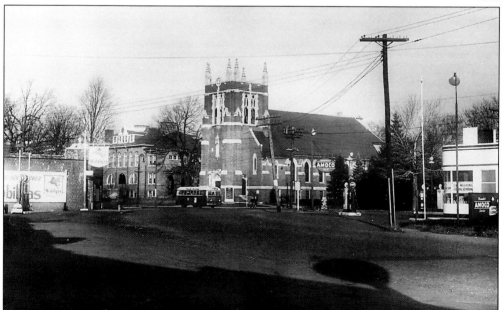

The fire-ravaged frame of St. Joseph's Church was quickly replaced by a large, cathedral-like brick structure that housed an expanding congregation. In 1952 the parish was divided and St. Bartholomew's was created. The current, modern, third St. Joseph's Church was built in the 1960s.

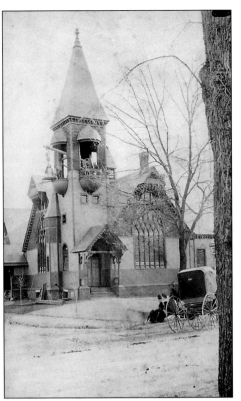

Pictured in 1890, this building was dedicated in 1889. It became the Evangelical Congregational church in 1897 and was later destroyed by fire. A new church structure was erected on the same site at Great Plain Avenue and Linden Street in 1925. Part of the 1925 building remains as Fellowship Hall, which was built on the same location in 1952 for the current Congregational Church (United Church of Christ).

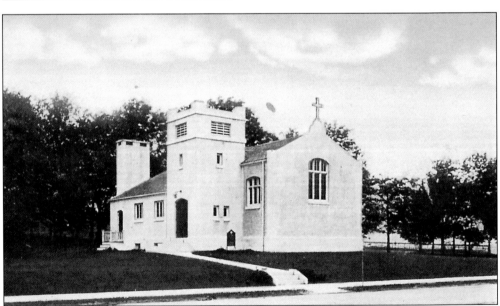

Christ Church Episcopal in Needham was incorporated in 1895 and met in a small frame building on Highland Avenue. This building was erected in 1912. William Carter promised to give the land to the parish if within a month it could pledge for construction an amount of money equal to his donation. The goal was accomplished. The 1912 building has been incorporated into a larger structure at the corner of Highland Avenue and Rosemary Street.

Six
Around Our Town

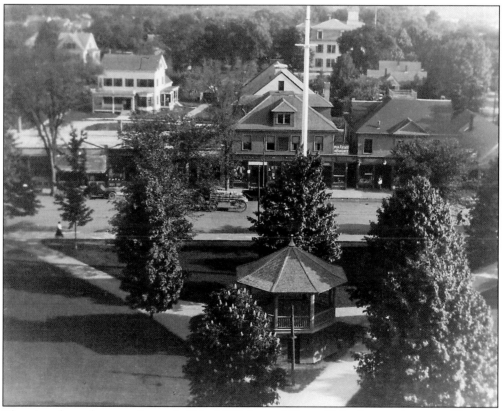

The view from the top of town hall in 1920 showed Great Plain Avenue between Chestnut Street and Dedham Avenue. A large house occupied what is now a parking lot. The Kimball School dominated the right background. On the town common was a bandstand, built in 1911 for $800. Moved to Memorial Park in 1924 and dismantled in 1940 because of decay, it was replaced with a gazebo by the Needham Exchange Club in 1985 for $20,000.

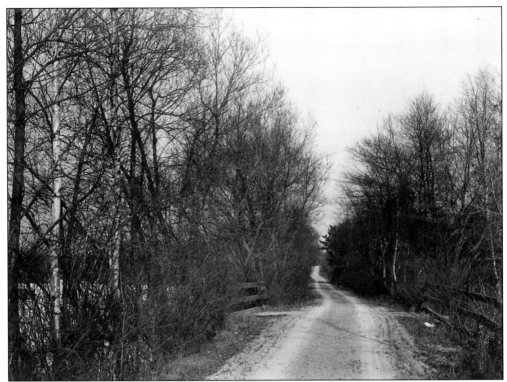
This rural scene of 1903 featured the road from Charles River Village to Dover. On the left of the one-lane, crude dirt road was the Charles River.

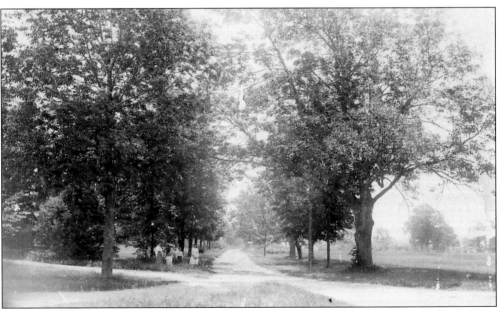
Until the late 1800s, the rural character of Needham was in evidence, even along Great Plain Avenue, shown here at the Webster Street crossing. Two youngsters and two women waited on the corner.

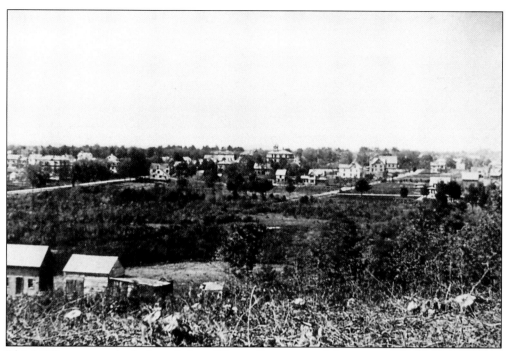

This 1888 panorama looked north from Warren Street toward the new center of Needham. The O'Keefe house was in the foreground.

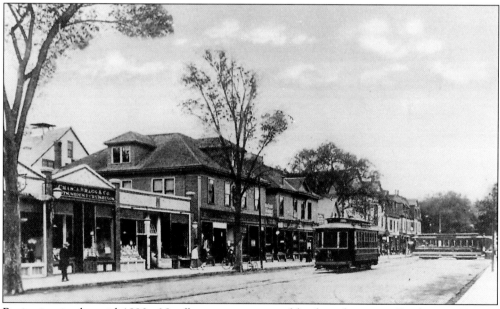

Beginning in the mid-1890s, Needham was connected by five electric trolley lines to Boston and our neighbors. We became a "trolley car suburb." In the center of the business district at Great Plain Avenue and Chestnut Street, the trolley in the foreground was moving on the Wellesley-Dedham line. In the background, a trolley moved on the Natick-Newton line. The last trolley in Needham ran in 1927 and was replaced by buses.

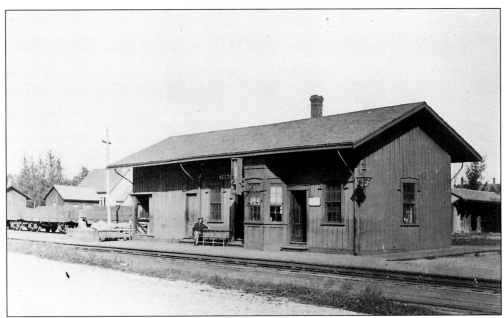

A railroad finally came to Needham in 1853—the Charles River Branch Railroad. It did not, however, come to East Needham along Central Avenue but was built onto the Great Plain. This eventually necessitated the removal of the town's business to the present center of town. This station stood in Needham Center prior to 1887 when it was lost in a fire.

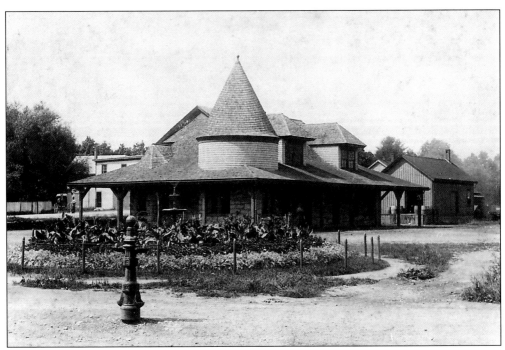

After the fire at the old Needham Center station, a large, stone railroad station was erected at the Great Plain Avenue crossing, a fragment of which still remains and is in use as a restaurant.

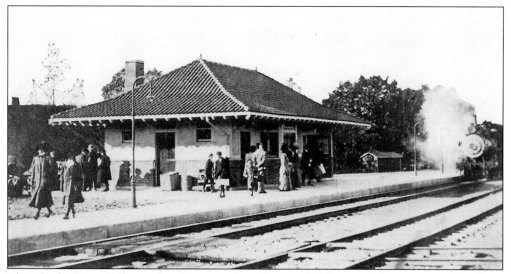

The Charles River Village railroad station, shown here in 1910, opened that section of Needham to business. The line, part of the New York, New England, and Erie Railroad, reached across Rhode Island and Connecticut. The building remained until the 1960s when train service to Medfield was discontinued.

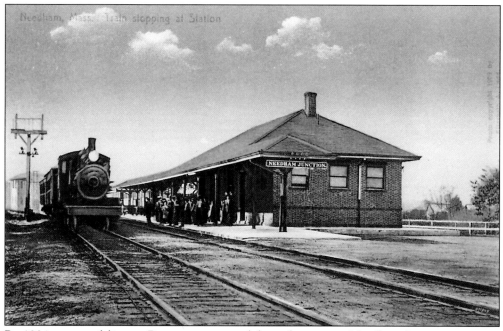

By 1904, a second line to Boston was created from the present Needham Junction, running through West Roxbury to Hyde Park. It eventually became the main line into Boston with more than sixty-five trains per day. Today it is a busy commuter route to Boston.

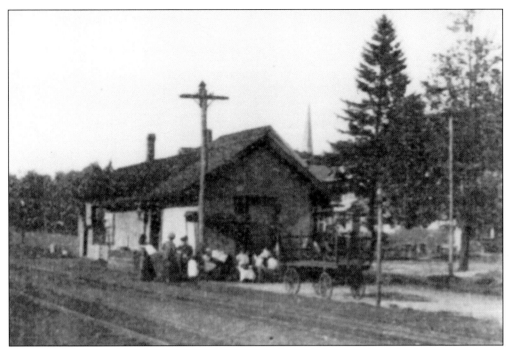

The establishment of freight service to Boston accelerated the growth of the knitting industry in Needham Heights. This was the Highlandville station. The line was also used after 1859 to cart Needham soil and gravel for Back Bay fill.

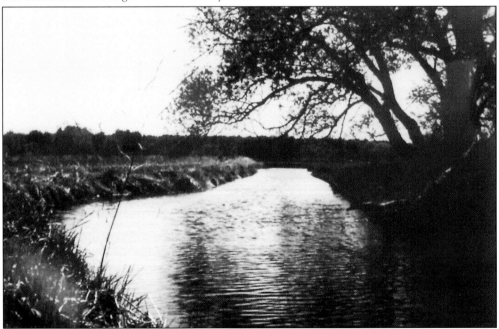

Needham's Great Ditch was dug in the seventeenth century by East Anglians who were familiar with the fens country of England. The Charles River meanders around three sides of Needham. This ditch cuts off some 3 miles of a big bend in the Charles between Needham and Dedham. It is still part of the eastern boundary of our town and is a punting canal.

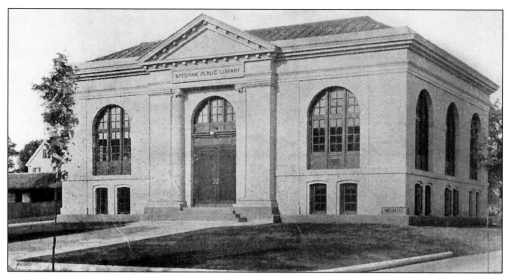

On land donated by William Carter and with funds supplied by Andrew Carnegie, the first public library building in Needham opened in 1904. This town had innumerable library resources from 1796 on, located in rooms in several business blocks. After the library moved in 1915, Carter acquired this building for a business office. It subsequently became a bank and was later razed for the construction of a drive-in bank facility.

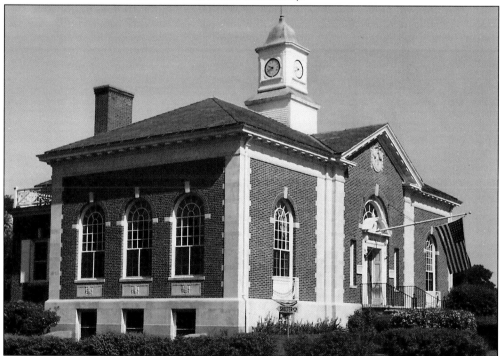

The library moved in 1915 because the town was unhappy with the location of the Carnegie Library in Highlandville. Again, on land donated by William Carter, the present Needham Free Public Library was built on the border between Needham Center and Highlandville at the corner of Highland Avenue and Rosemary Street. The building was enlarged in 1961 with expanded facilities for students and the general reading public.

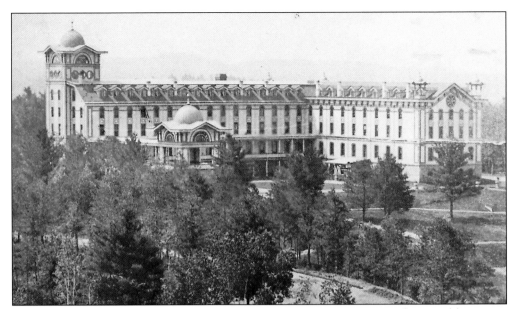

The Baker Estate or Ridge Hill Farms in Needham was an amusement park created by sewing machine magnate William Emerson Baker on some 750 acres near Grove and Charles River Streets. In 1877 Baker shipped the Great American Restaurant Building to Needham from the 1876 Philadelphia Centennial. This became Hotel Wellesley with two hundred guestrooms, stables for one hundred horses, a dining room seating six hundred, bowling alleys, and a boathouse.

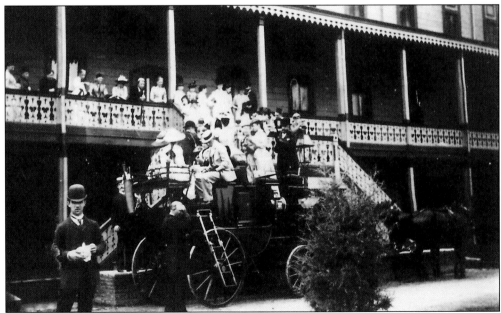

Guests arrived by coach at Hotel Wellesley, open only from June to October. A railroad spur connected the hotel to the Charles River Village station. The hotel was operated and staffed by personnel of the Massachusetts Institute of Cookery in Boston. Its appointments were reported to be "first class." Never a commercial success, the hotel burned down in 1891, having been in operation during twelve summers. It was never rebuilt.

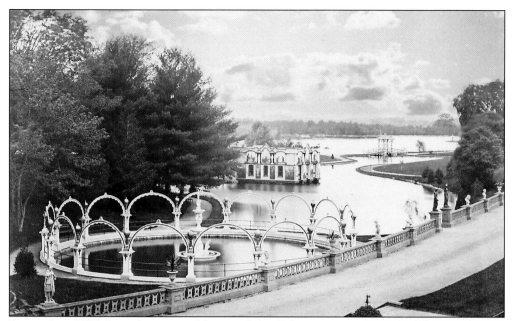

Pictured in 1885 from the terraced lawns of the Baker estate, man-made Sabrina Lake was decorated with a spray fountain, a white and gold boathouse storing rowboats and canoes, and a rustic bridge. By diverting streams, building dikes, and excavating springs, Baker constructed this lake, which had a circumference of 1.5 miles, and stocked it with game fish. Private homes now border on Sabrina Lake.

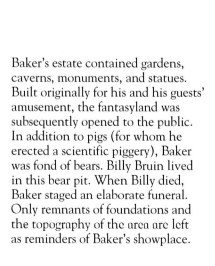

Baker's estate contained gardens, caverns, monuments, and statues. Built originally for his and his guests' amusement, the fantasyland was subsequently opened to the public. In addition to pigs (for whom he erected a scientific piggery), Baker was fond of bears. Billy Bruin lived in this bear pit. When Billy died, Baker staged an elaborate funeral. Only remnants of foundations and the topography of the area are left as reminders of Baker's showplace.

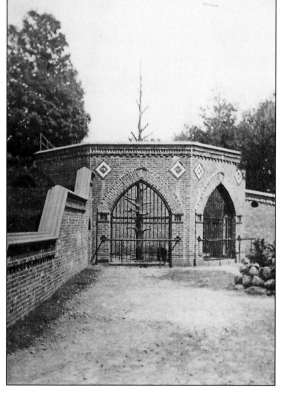

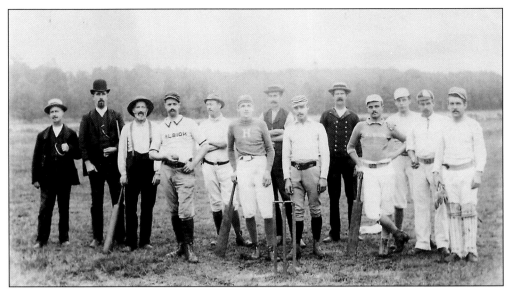

The Albion Cricket Club of Highlandville was the East Coast champion in the 1890s and reflected the English character of the knitting industry in town. Needham was called "the cricket capitol of Massachusetts." The club was one of several such organizations enjoyed by the English-Scotch residents and was financially supported by William Carter, who also gave to Needham its cricket field in his beloved Needham Heights section.

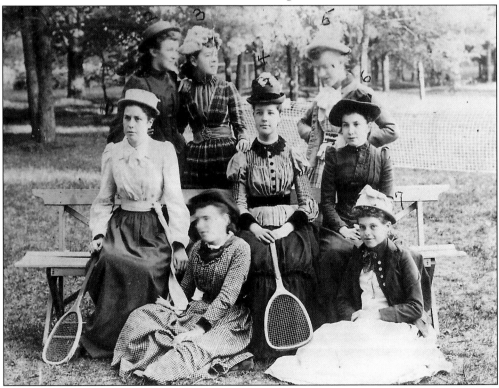

By the turn of the century, Needham's women were becoming active in sports. These "appropriately garbed" ladies waited with rackets for the game to begin.

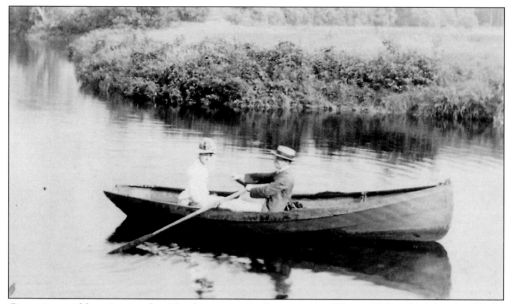

Canoeing and boating on the Charles were popular sports, as Mr. and Mrs. C. Atherton Hicks demonstrated. The more than 11 miles of the Charles River almost encircling Needham have always lent themselves to boating, fishing, and swimming. There were boat rental facilities in several locations, such as Red Wing Bay in the Charles River Village section and the Highland Avenue Bridge in Needham Heights.

In 1936, Needham sent five participants (four men and one woman) to the Olympic Games in Berlin, Germany. They competed in track, field, and rowing events. This newspaper spread is included in the exhibit at the Needham Historical Society featuring our sports history.

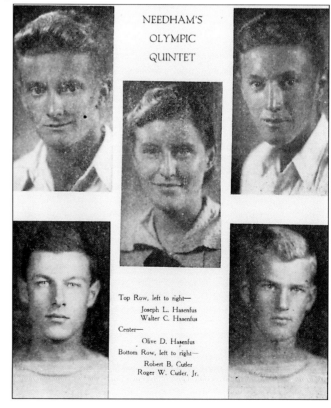

NEEDHAM'S OLYMPIC QUINTET

Top Row, left to right—
Joseph L. Hasenfus
Walter C. Hasenfus
Center—
Olive D. Hasenfus
Bottom Row, left to right—
Robert B. Cutler
Roger W. Cutler, Jr.

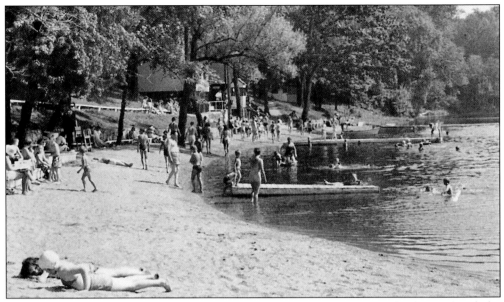

Rosemary Lake is fed by Rosemary Creek and underground streams. When the dam is closed, the lake fills. For decades Rosemary Beach was used for swimming by thousands each summer. When the lake became polluted, Rosemary Pool was built along the shore and uniquely submerged in the lake. It remains a favorite summer spot for residents and is part of our extensive park and recreation department sports program.

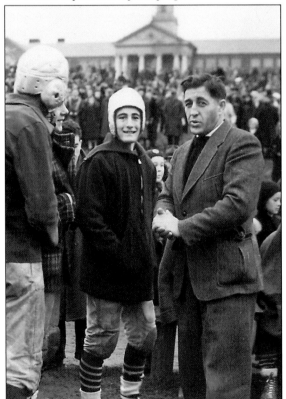

From the 1930s into the 1960s, Philip Claxton (at right) coached at Needham High School, created our park and recreation program, and organized Little League Baseball and Pee Wee Football. Claxton coached many Needham-Wellesley football games, which represent the oldest secondary school football rivalry in the country, dating back over one hundred years. A major sports field in town honors Claxton's name and accomplishments.

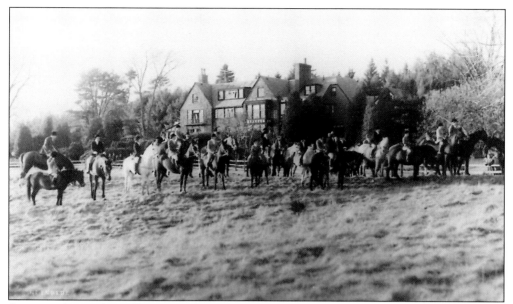

Some residents of Needham's "Gold Coast" along South Street participated in fox hunting. Here the Norfolk Hunt prepared to "ride to the hounds" on the lawn of the Noel Morss estate. At the end of the run, a hunt breakfast was held.

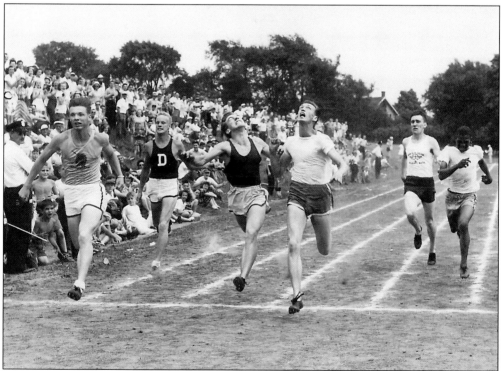

New England Amateur Athletic Union (NEAAU) track meets were held in Needham during many July Fourth celebrations in the 1950s. These were often qualifying meets for national and Olympic competitions, held on one of the finest running tracks in the country—Memorial Field.

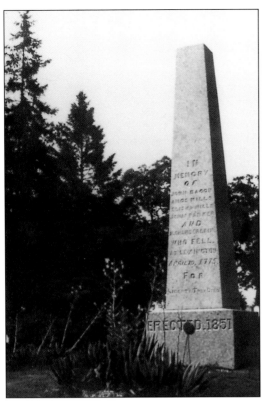

In the old cemetery on Nehoiden Street, the Ladies Aid Society of the First Parish Church erected a monument to the five Needham militiamen who were killed in the Battle of Menotomy (Arlington) during the retreat of the British from Lexington and Concord. The men left five widows and twenty-eight children. The monument is a Quincy granite, four-sided obelisk with the chiseled inscription, "For Liberty They Died."

Dedicated in 1902, our Civil War Soldiers' Monument stands in Needham Cemetery on a lot purchased by the local G.A.R. Post 181. It is the centerpiece of the veterans' section of the cemetery. The four, 32-pound naval guns and sixty cannon balls were "loaned" by the 57th United States Congress. Annual Memorial Day exercises are held at the site. More than four hundred Needham residents served in the Civil War.

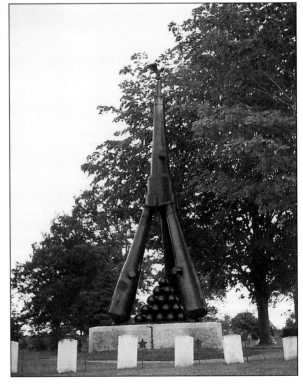

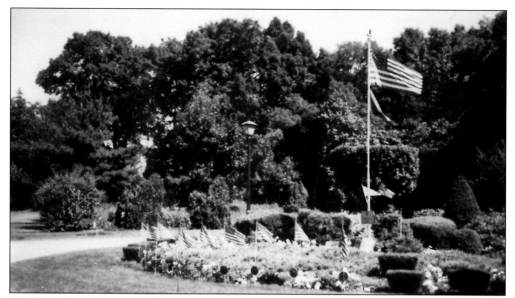

Needham has not forgotten her Vietnam War participants. Developed and maintained by Tony Cefalo, this site was dedicated in 1984 and is located off Central Avenue on Sunset Road. Nine Needham residents lost their lives in Vietnam.

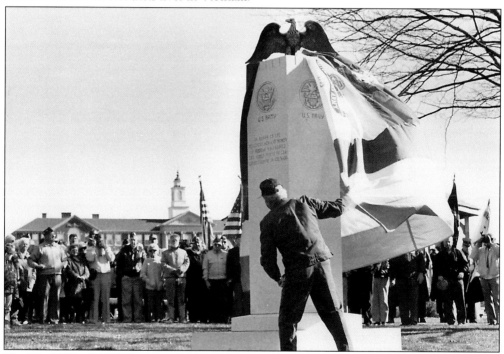

The World War II 50th Anniversary Commemoration included the dedication of a monument at Memorial Park. The Veteran's Memorial Committee collected funds for the pentagonal granite pillar, topped with a bronze eagle, each side honoring a branch of the United States military. The monument was unveiled on Veterans Day 1995, "IN HONOR OF THE DEDICATED MEN AND WOMEN OF NEEDHAM WHO SERVED IN THE ARMED FORCES OF OUR COUNTRY IN ALL WARS."

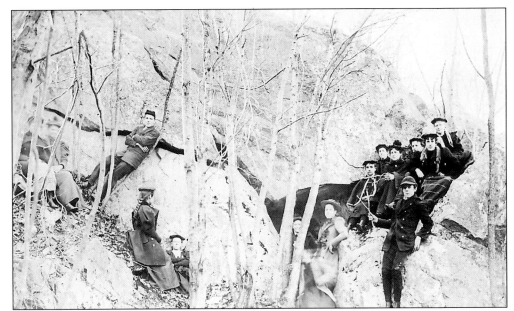

Devil's Den in the High Rock Woods of the Needham Town Forest was supposedly a shelter used by wild animals. Since the nineteenth century, the area has been a popular hiking and picnic spot and a place for mysterious adventures for many youngsters. For several years, a Boy Scout camp was located nearby.

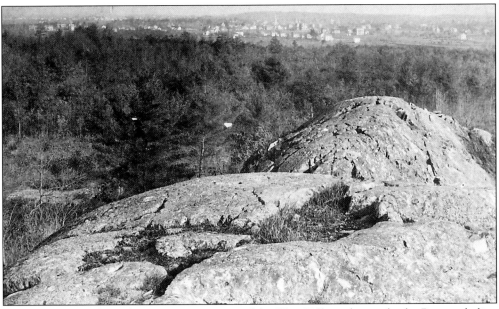

Seen from the High Rock is a panoramic view of the Blue Hills to the south, the Boston skyline to the east, and the town of Needham. Since the 1930s, the surrounding area has been preserved as the Needham Town Forest and includes a skating pond and interesting hiking trails. For many years, a small shack in the woods nearby was the home of a gentleman who chose to live a hermit's life.

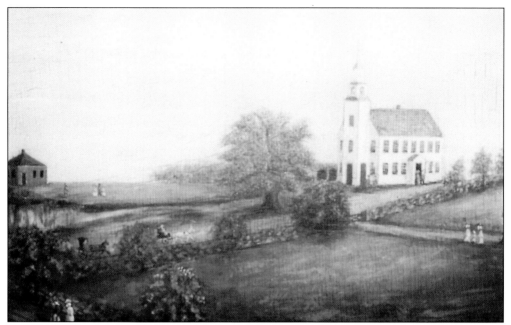

Known as "the Centre" in the early 1800s, Needham's civic center was located on Central Avenue between Great Plain Avenue and Nehoiden Street. This early-nineteenth-century painting by Lucius Newell, now at the Needham Historical Society, shows the area with the little brick schoolhouse at left and the second meetinghouse and Nehoiden Street at right.

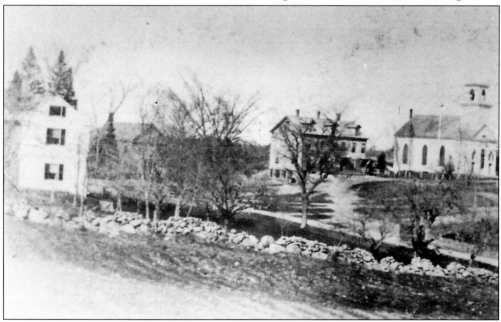

Perhaps the oldest extant photograph (c. 1870) of a Needham scene shows the old town "centre" pre-1879, with the third meetinghouse (or First Parish Church) in its original location. Left of the church was Revere's store and Nehoiden Hall, later moved to Rosemary Street and used as a tenement. The militia training field was behind the church and store. The Davis Mills house (now North Hill Farm) is at the left.

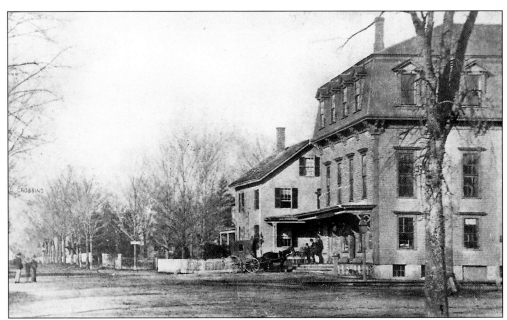

Built in 1854, this building was first the Stephen Harvey Block and Village Hall, the first store block and social hall built in Great Plain Village. Pictured in 1874, it stood on the site now occupied by a bank east of Garden Street at the railroad tracks. The building became known as Parker Hall when purchased by Obed Parker of Nantucket. It was destroyed by fire in 1882.

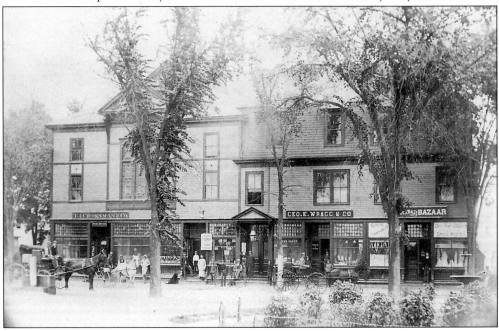

The structure at the southwest corner of Great Plain Avenue and Chestnut Street was known at various times as the Moseley, May, or Bourne Block. Pictured c. 1885, it had six stores and a post office on the first floor, with an auditorium, meeting room, and police lockup above. This 1874 building was taken down in 1928 and replaced with the current one-story block. In the foreground were the flower garden and fountain of the railroad station.

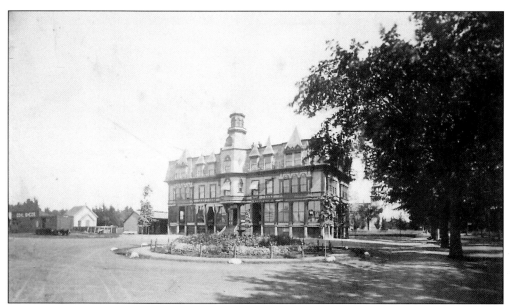

Located at Great Plain Avenue and Chapel Street, the Odd Fellows Building was a major business edifice. It was destroyed by fire in 1887 and this site remained vacant until 1928. Arson was suspected and a $500 reward offered to find the perpetrator. The building housed the library, an auditorium, the G.A.R. headquarters, and professional offices on the top floors with a milliner, a shoe store, a steam printer, and a market below.

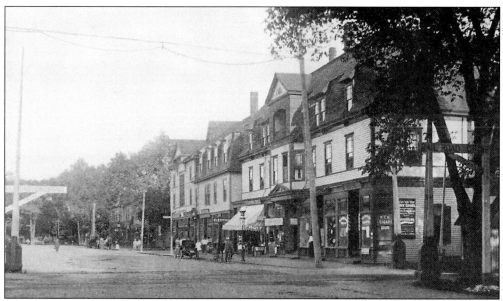

Built in 1887 on Great Plain Avenue at the railroad tracks, the Kingsbury Block (foreground) was destroyed by fire in 1980 and replaced in 1983 with a three-story brick building. Named for an early Needham family, it housed a large auditorium used after the Odd Fellows auditorium was destroyed and meeting rooms where the town's many social and fraternal organizations gathered. William Jennings Bryan spoke and Chautauquas met there.

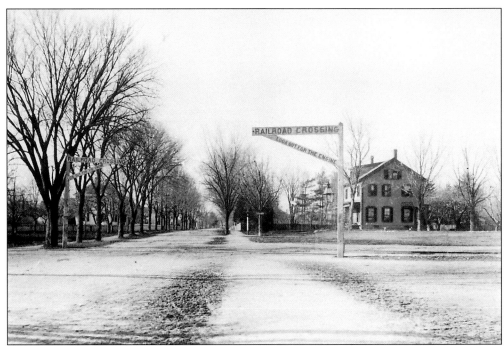

In Needham Center in 1879 there was a house on Great Plain Avenue approximately on the site where two bank buildings have been located in recent years.

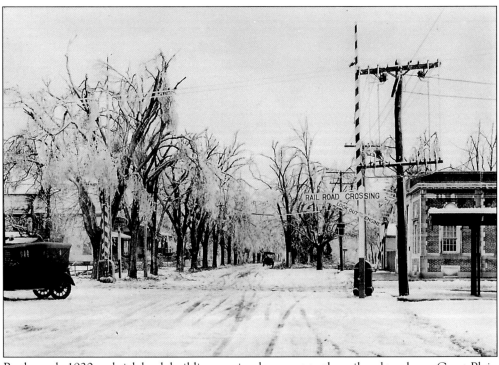

By the early 1920s, a brick bank building was in place next to the railroad tracks on Great Plain Avenue. This was the bank that was robbed in the 1934 Needham bank heist.

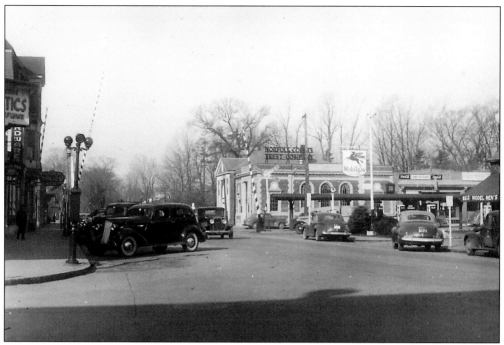

By 1942, the same area in downtown Needham was the site of a bustling commercial scene. Angle parking was in style. The overhang for the railroad waiting area (at right) extended to the Great Plain Avenue sidewalk. A restaurant occupied the space behind the bank and a gas station was in business.

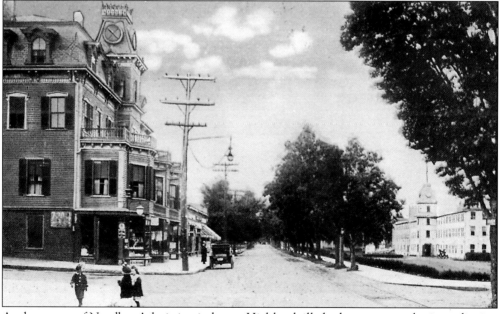

As the center of Needham's knitting industry, Highlandville had a prosperous business district. In 1907 the area was renamed Needham Heights. The large building at the left was located on Highland Avenue at West Street. The William Carter Company was on the right. Trolley tracks connected Needham and Newton.

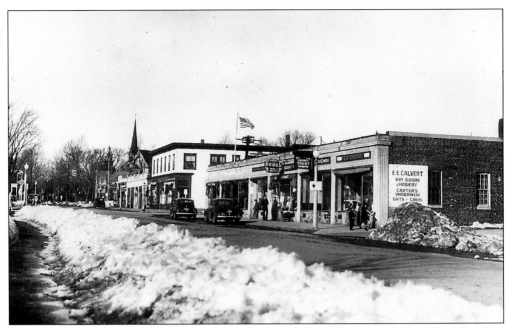

The Needham Heights business district in 1942 included the one-story building that had replaced the larger towered structure at the corner of West Street and Highland Avenue. E.E. Calvert's small dry goods store, on the right of the block, was an outlet for Carter's underwear. Calvert's expanded over the years to fill the entire block and was a good source of clothes for growing families until it closed in 1995.

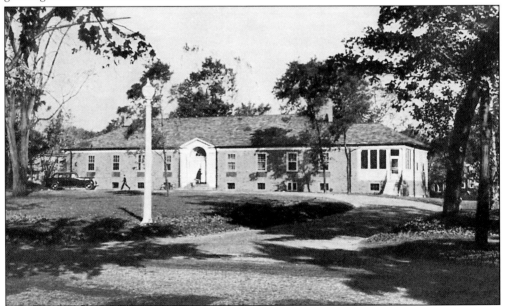

In 1910, the Glover Home and Hospital opened on property at Chestnut and Lincoln Streets donated by Frederick Glover, farmer and selectman. Glover's former home was the hospital building. In 1936, the nucleus of the modern hospital was constructed and named Glover Memorial in honor of Needham's World War I dead. The hospital was enlarged in the 1970s and recently became part of the Deaconess Hospital System.

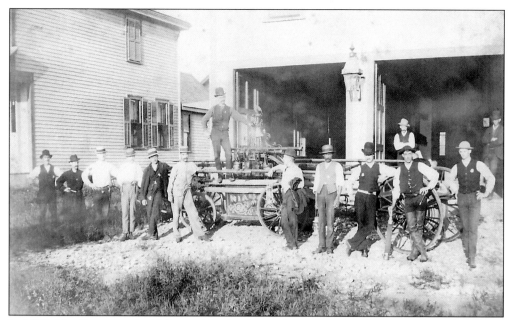

In 1884, Needham acquired Niagara No. 1, a horse-drawn, two-hand pumper. It was housed in local barns before a station was built on Chestnut Street across from the current fire headquarters. In 1916, Niagara was sold for the copper scrap in its water tank. At the time of the Odd Fellows Building fire, Niagara's men saved the Moseley Building across the street, using water from a cistern at the town drinking fountain.

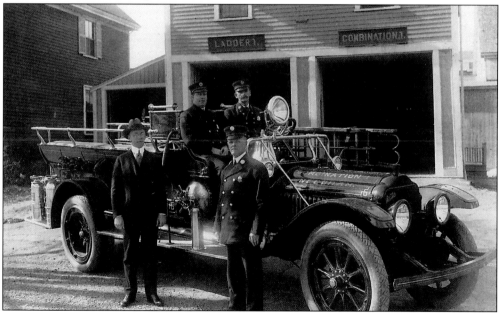

In 1916, Needham bought its first motorized fire apparatus, Combination No. 1, assuring faster response time. The apparatus had a 40-gallon chemical tank and several ladders. Two permanent firemen were placed at Station 1 in the center. Prior to this, the fire company was all volunteer. Telephones were installed in the station and sleeping rooms were provided for the firefighters. Volunteer help was still used, with fines levied for absence from fires.

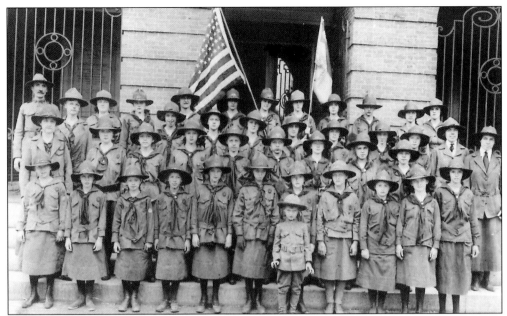

The Red Rose Troop, organized in 1917, was the first Girl Scout troop in Needham. Meeting first in the town hall, membership grew so rapidly that within a year the troop was subdivided and met in various churches. During World War I, the troop rolled bandages, packed nursing equipment, and knit sweaters for soldiers. Needham Girl Scouts marched in one of the nation's first drum and bugle corps.

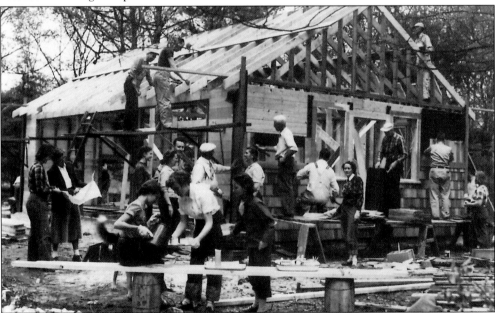

In 1952, volunteers added a shelter building to Camp Malcolm, a local Girl Scout day camp. In 1927, Mr. and Mrs. James McCracken donated a portion of their property off Nehoiden Street and a camp house for scout activities. Camp Malcolm was named for a McCracken son who died at age ten, and the memorial has been enjoyed by thousands over the years. Troops hiked to the camp and used adjacent Rosemary Lake for swimming and canoeing.

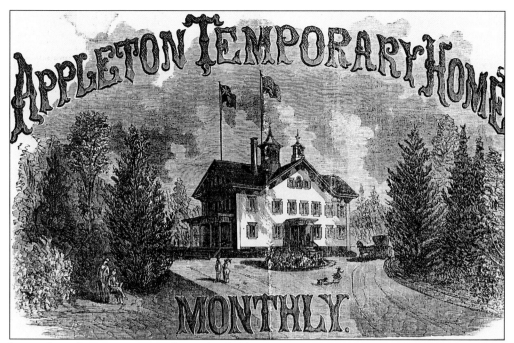

Located in a former private academy, the Oakland Institute at May Street and Oakland Avenue, the Appleton Temporary Home for Inebriates was established for the moral and scientific treatment of alcoholism in men. Originating under the auspices of the Temperance Society of the Boston Young Men's Christian Association in 1872, it became a private institution and was in operation until 1881.

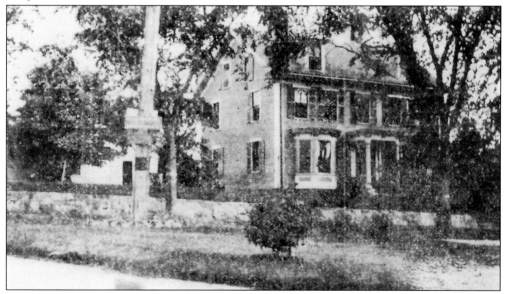

Publicized as a place "where tired mothers with their little ones may go from the city for a two weeks rest," Mother's Rest was at West Street and Greendale Avenue. Started in 1900 by a Baptist minister, the enterprise was taken over by an interdenominational association that purchased the estate. Discouraged women who attended were "sent home full of hope and courage" and "puny, sickly babies were brought back to health."

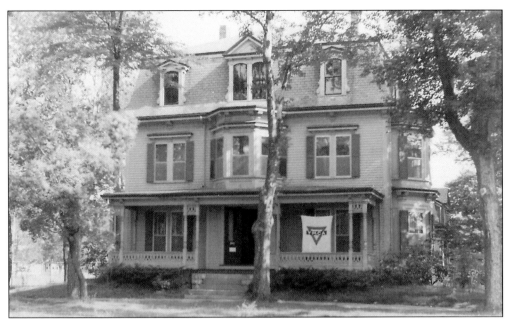

A Young Men's Christian Association group was formed in Needham in 1880, sponsored by the Methodist Episcopal church in Highlandville. For many years, the group met in rooms in the Moseley and Kingsbury Blocks. The current location in the 1880s home once owned by Dr. David Mann on Great Plain Avenue contains a swimming pool used for Y training sessions and high school swimming practices.

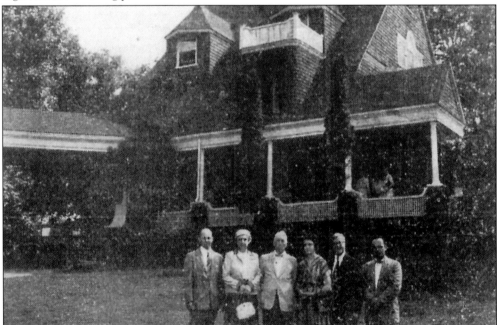

In 1952, the George H. and Irene L. Walker Home for Children, on Central Avenue near Dover, was dedicated. The home, an estate house on the former Walker-Gordon Farm, had been renovated and was ready for the care of children in need. The facility continues its work today.

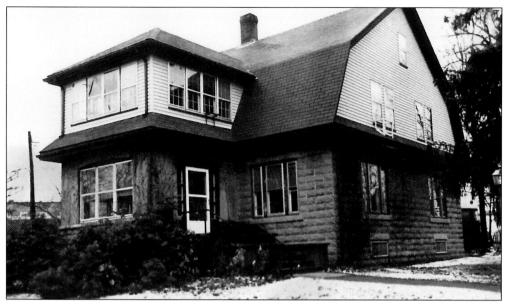

The Needham Community Council is a volunteer, non-profit organization that acts as a coordinator for our social agencies. Located since 1950 in a former residence on Lincoln Street, the council focuses community spirit on valuable social programs such as a food pantry, a clothing exchange, a medical equipment lending service, a widowed-to-widowed program, a senior citizens' transportation service, a "friendly visitors" program, a literacy program, and a homemaker program.

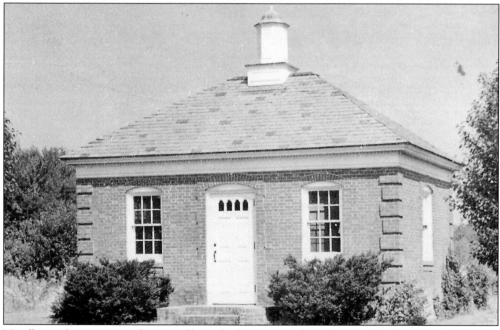

Needham obtains most of its excellent drinking water from deep wells that were dug in the late 1930s off Charles River Street near the river crossing into South Natick. When dug, they were the deepest man-made wells in the world. The pumping station handles an average of 2.5 million gallons of water per day.

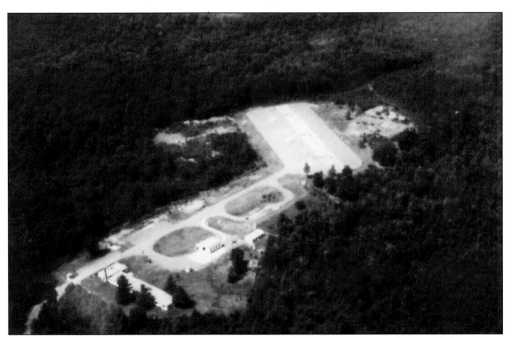

During the 1950s, Needham became a location of one of the many Nike guided missile launching sites that protected Greater Boston. The headquarters and control center of the operation were situated at the top of North Hill, as was housing for personnel. The silos shown here were located off Pine Street. Each silo extended 50 feet underground.

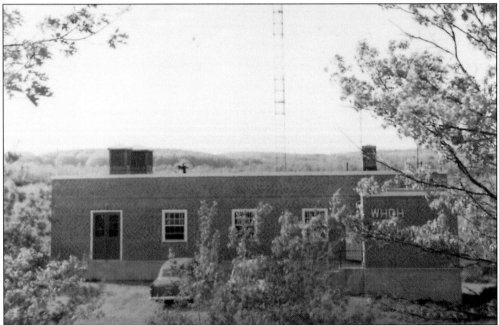

Needham is a communications center for Greater Boston. From the 1930s, sites in town have served as transmission points for many radio and television stations because Needham sits on the highest elevation between Boston and Rhode Island. WHDH radio, located off Central Avenue near the Needham Pool and Racquet Club, is one such station.

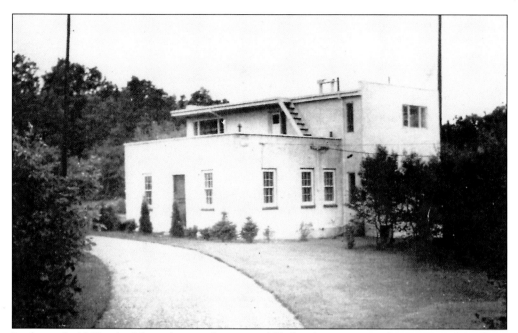

In the early 1940s, the Massachusetts Institute of Technology sponsored a project in Needham after a one-year search for a site. The Laboratory for Cosmic Terrestrial Research was located on Bird Street in a sparsely settled district with unusually good radio reception. The purpose of the project was "the observation and accumulation of geophysical data pertaining to the action, reaction and interaction of cosmic- and geo-phenomena."

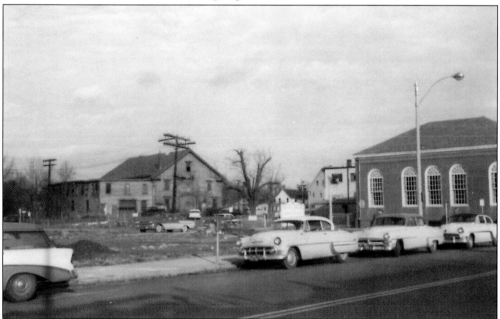

In December 1959, construction was underway in an area along Great Plain Avenue at Garden Street. This had originally been the site of houses. On this plot, the business block now housing Bergson's Ice Cream was built. In the background was the old Eaton Livery Stable and Barn, which was later taken down.

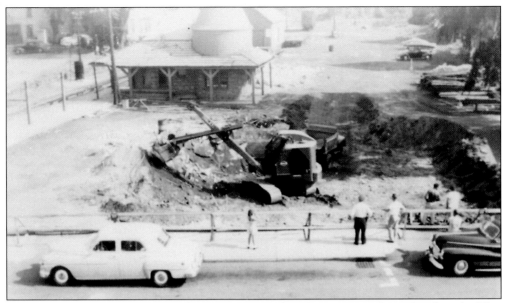

In 1950, new construction was underway on Great Plain Avenue near the railroad tracks. This area was open space and was an entrance leading to the Needham Center train station at the rear. Built on the site was the business block now housing a Chinese restaurant and a paint store on the left and a camera shop on the right.

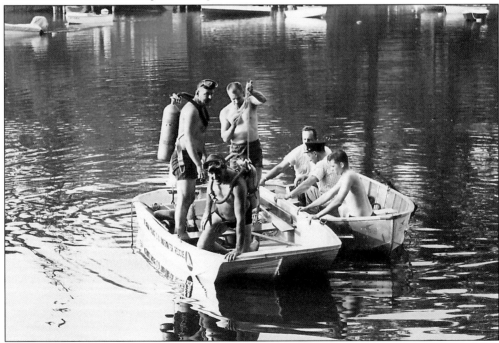

The Needham police force of the 1880s consisted of public-spirited volunteers, constables, and special-duty night watchmen. After the first police chief was appointed in 1899, the department kept pace with the needs of our growing community. Training is vital for the modern police force. Because of Rosemary Lake and the Charles River, which encompasses Needham on three sides, underwater rescue training has been important for our skilled policemen.

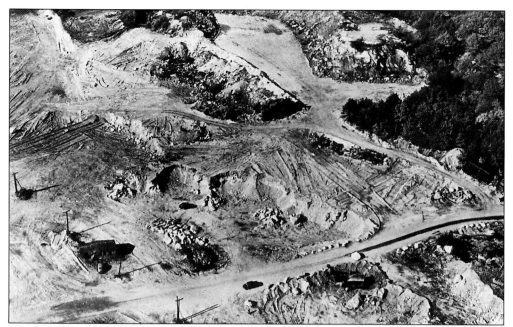

Before its development by Cabot, Cabot & Forbes as the Needham Industrial Center, this area along Route 128 was virtually a desert from which billowing waves of dust often blew toward Needham Center. This condition was created when the area was used as the major source of the fill that was taken into Boston to construct the Back Bay.

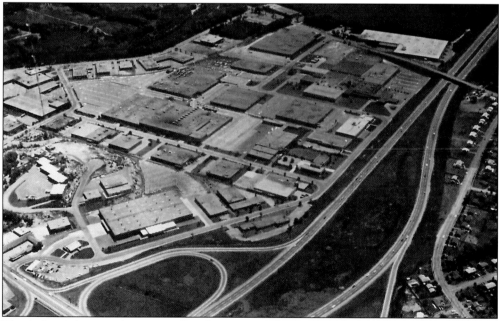

The industrial center houses small industries and the nation's largest Coca-Cola plant. The location of the new Route 128 was a key element in the success of the center. A railroad spur was built into the area in the 1950s and the quickly sold-out development helped to stabilize Needham's tax rate after a period of 25 percent population growth and a ten-times increase in municipal debt.

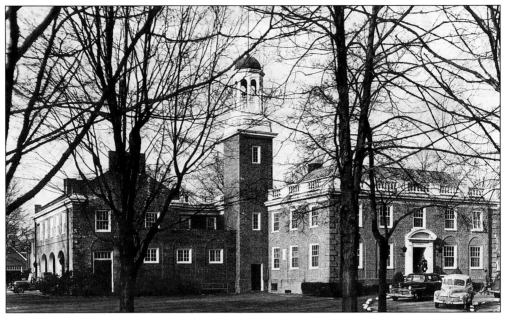

Our police and fire departments have shared this Georgian Colonial-style building at Chestnut and School Streets since 1932. Earlier fire stations stood across the street from this building, at Charles River Village, and at Needham Heights, where a station remains. The police lockup occupied part of the Moseley Block in the early days and from 1911 to 1932 was located in town hall.

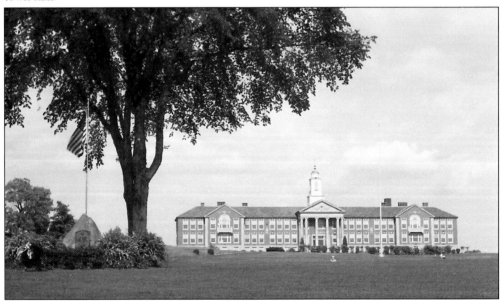

Overlooking Memorial Park stands Needham High School, crown jewel of our public education system, built in 1929, later enlarged several times, and renovated recently in a $6 million project. The rural quality of Needham has disappeared, businesses have changed, residents have arrived from around the world, and architecture has become more varied. This building, however, still stands proudly as a symbol of hope for the future through the lives of the students nurtured here.